MILLENNIUM DIARY

As this book goes to print in August 1999 Downton is planning to celebrate
These are the events we know about

1999

Downton Churches Together will deliver an Advent Candle and Prayer to every home. It is hoped they will be lit in every household at midnight on 31 December where household members are gathered.

31 December	NEW YEAR'S EVE PARTY and MILLENNIUM FIREWORKS. **Downton Leisure Centre 8.00pm.** OPEN SERVICE at **St Laurence Church 11.45 pm.** Everyone welcome GUILD OF BELLRINGERS 'Ring out the old and ring in the new millennium'

2000

2 January	JOINT VILLAGE SERVICE. **St Laurence Church 10.00 am.**
12 February	CHILDREN'S DISCO. **Memorial Hall.** To choose the Carnival Princess and attendants.
29 April	THE CUCKOO FAIR. **The Borough 10.00 am to 4.00 pm.**
1 May	TABLE TOP SALE & REFRESHMENTS. **Memorial Hall 10.00 am.** Wessex Cancer Trust.
6 & 7 May	"THE PRODIGAL SON" **St Laurence Church** A new musical written by Miranda Whitehead, produced by Peter Waddington and Downton Pageant Productions.
20 May	SPRING PLANT SALE. **Memorial Hall 2.00 pm to 5.00 pm.** Downton Horticultural Society. BARFORD DAY CENTRE CONCERT PARTY. To be arranged.
17 June	**DOWNTON VILLAGE MILLENNIUM CARNIVAL**
1.00 pm	Starts at **Wick Lane**, procession moves through village to **Barford Lane rugby field.**
5.00 pm to 7.00 pm	**Memorial Gardens** CEILIDH
7.00 pm to 8.00 pm	**Memorial Gardens** BRIAN MOON AND THE SATELLITES
8.00 pm	**Memorial Gardens** MILLENNIUM CONCERT Music and dance tell the story of the last 100 years
24 June	SUMMER SHOW **Memorial Hall 2.00 pm to 5.00 pm** Downton Horticultural Society
7 July	SUMMER PARTY **New Court** Downton Society
8 July	**Millennium Green from 10.00 am** Teddy Bears' Picnic, view the Millennium Sun Clock - have fun!
26 July	COFFEE MORNING **Chalkhill House 10.30 am** Barford Day Centre
2 September	AUTUMN FLOWER SHOW **Memorial Hall 2.00 pm to 5.00 pm** Downton Horticultural Society
30 September	MILLENNIUM CONCERT **Memorial Hall** Downton Band
28 October	TABLE TOP SALE **Memorial Hall 10.00 am** Wessex Cancer Trust
12 November	REMEMBRANCE SUNDAY PARADE AND SERVICE **Memorial Hall and St Laurence Church** Royal British Legion
4 December	WHIST DRIVE **Memorial Hall** Downton Horticultural Society

DOWNTON
7000 years of an
English Village

Author: **David Waymouth**

Illustrator: **Jane Ancona**

Designer: **Geoffrey Holland**

Published by **Downton Millennial Book Fund**

This first edition published in 1999 by
Downton Millennial Book Fund

Illustrator:
Jane Ancona
Orchards, Quavey Road, REDLYNCH SP5 2HH

Designer:
Geoff Holland
G&A GRAPHICS, 3 Joanna Close, DOWNTON SP5 3NP. *Tel:* 01725 513132

Printed and bound by
The Cromwell Press
Aintree Avenue, White Horse Business Park, TROWBRIDGE BA14 0XB

Millennium Commission

The Millennium Festival Fund provided some of the money needed to publish this book; all profits go to Downton village charities.

ISBN 0-9536109-0-X *Hardback*
ISBN 0-9536109-1-8 *Paperback*
ISBN 0-9536109-2-6 *Leatherbound*

CONTENTS

Downton's Millennial Programme

The Downton Hundred contains 'Dunckton' which is Downton today

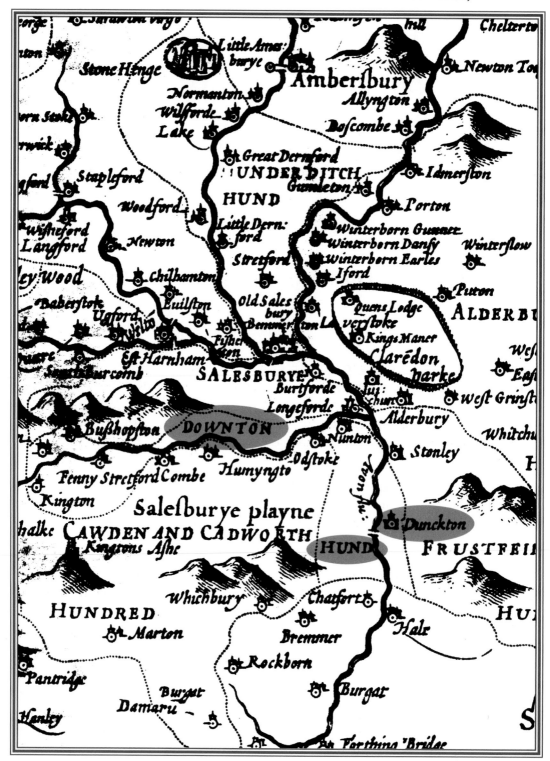

Part of Wiltshire Map 1610

DOWNTON

7000 years of an

English Village

PREAMBLE

Another Downton Millennium Ends

CELEBRATING IN STYLE

It is April 1998. Downton is to have a party. A big party. A year-long party to mark a new Millennium. The people who will help it happen are meeting. Beer and sandwiches at the ready. Upwards of thirty of them, builder and baker, squire and vicar, old and young, in-comers and those who were born in the village, Top-enders and Bottom-enders - all have come with ideas and offers of help.

'Carnival - Irish ceilidh - bonfire and fireworks - rustic sports - open air concert and pageant - discos and dances - and, perhaps best of all, a New Year's Eve party for the whole family together' come surging out with much banter and laughter. Nearly two years away but already the party mood is on Downton.

A MILLENNIUM MARKER

As this team plan to celebrate the start of a new Millennium probably most are only vaguely aware of how many other celebrations there have been in Downton over its many centuries. Coronations and Jubilees, great victories and declarations of peace, elections, even the passing of great reforms have all been excuses for this friendly village to let its hair down.

This book aims to bring alive the happiness and the hardship of a village that goes back a long, long way. It sets out to do it in several ways. There are the historical facts about Downton as far as we know them. There are little playlets inspired and loosely based on those written by Dr Miranda Whitehead for the 1994 Downton Pageant. There are pictures and maps and lists and tables, there are little nuggets that are meant to be fun or helpful. There are guides on what to look for

1

Preamble Another Downton Millennium Ends

as you walk through the village and round the church. Together we hope they give a living, moving feel for Downton as it is today.

This is no work of scholarship. There is some guesswork and plenty of generous interpretation of known facts. We hope it can give both those who already know and love Downton and those coming to it for the first time a sense of continuity. We want you to enjoy a marvellous heritage, the real story of England.

Downton loves a party .....

WITH ACKNOWLEDGEMENTS TO ROWLANDSON

Chapter 1

The First Men in Downton

Downton is a very ancient Wiltshire village, six miles south of Salisbury. People have lived here for over 7,000 years because it was and is a good place to live. It lies between two lines of chalk hills. It has a river, the Avon, which provided fresh water, fish, transport and lush meadows. It had plentiful game and plenty of good timber. Above all else it was a place where men and animals could cross the river and its hard gravel ford was the best for miles.

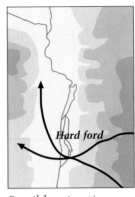

Possible migration routes

MAN ARRIVES

400,000 years ago herds of musk ox and elk made seasonal migrations across the dry land that is now the English Channel. Some of the very first men to venture in to England followed and lived off those herds. They might also have encountered elephant, rhino and monkeys. Finds of their stone tools show that they camped at Woodgreen, just south of Downton, before moving on up the river to Milford Hill, Salisbury. From there some went farther north to Salisbury Plain and to the Vale of Pewsey.

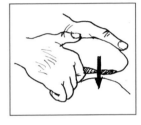

Flint knapping - progression of flakes

They were skilled makers of stone and flint axes and scrapers. They fished as well as hunted and they were happy living by water. The valley bottom was, however, twenty to thirty feet higher than now so it is not too surprising if we have few traces of their time here. Whether Downton was already a place where they camped because it was where the herds forded the river we do not know. Only one of their flint axes has been found near the village so far.

ICE AGES END

Except for a spell 20,000 years ago when the Ice Ages gripped the whole of Britain and drove man back across the land bridge to France, our ancestors continued to live all over southern England. As the ice retreated at the end of the last Ice Age, 8,000 years ago, so the herds of wild bison,

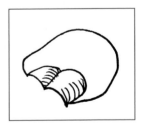

cattle, horses, red deer and elk would have once again been plentiful. They would have grazed on the savannah of Salisbury Plain rather as the cattle and ponies do today in the New Forest. As the herds moved south in the autumn and returned in the summer, small bands of hunters, each perhaps no more than 15 strong, moved with them. There may not have been more than 150 of these ancient people in the whole area.

OUR GENE POOL

Recent analysis of the DNA of one of these ancestral men found in a cave in Cheddar gorge showed him to be quite closely related genetically to modern men living in that area today. Other DNA tests show that most of us in Britain can trace our ancestry back to the earliest settlers - waves of Celts and Romans, Saxons and Normans seem to have done little to dilute the original gene pool already here.

SETTLEMENT 7,000 YEARS AGO

By 5,000 BC Downton would have been one of the places where the herds crossed the River Avon. When the sea rose to cut the land bridge to France 6,000 years ago with a final catastrophic flood as the melt water in the North Sea broke the link between Dover and Calais, so the annual migrations would have ceased and a more static life was possible. Gradually our forbears tamed and herded the wild cattle, horses, reindeer and even pigs. Their diet was higher in protein than ours today. That shows how much milk they drank and meat they ate.

In Downton their earliest homesteads were built in Castle Meadow over 7,000 years ago. This ledge of well-drained gravel with a good view right across the valley was a safe, dry place to camp near the ford.

We know this from excavations in 1956-7 that showed a few post holes round a shallow circular depression. The posts were to carry a lean-to or flimsy roof of skins or thatch and the pit was dug out to provide a surrounding bank built up to the roof as a shelter from wind and intruders.

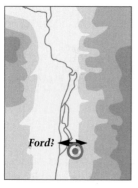

Ford?

⊙ *Mesolithic shelter and flints; Neolithic huts*

Such flimsy huts would protect the occupants from wolves, jackals and even bears by night at least long enough for warriors to rouse. Although much warmer as the ice withdrew to the north, the climate was probably colder and wetter than now. It would be a good dry place to leave babies and stores by day, guarded by the elderly. Associated flint tools, evidence of fire pits and animal remains suggest it was seasonal shelter for hunter-gatherers or herdsmen. Much the same shelters can still be seen in use by Kalahari and Masai tribesmen in Africa today.

An accident of cultural priorities and practical needs meant that none of the main development of Downton disturbed these ancient home sites until mains water and drains were available. By then their descendants could recognise their ancestors' old homes and cherish them.

Until the 1950's there were only three or four houses down Moot Lane. One important reason was that digging a well in that gravel is harder than elsewhere. So, in Downton we know where the first settlers lived and a little of their pattern of life.

Digging

Scraping

Skinning

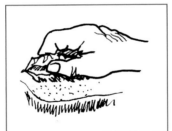

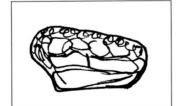
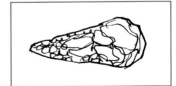

Along Moot Lane in Castle Meadow the remains of a Mesolithic circular shelter dating from 5,250 BC were found. The archaeological dig yielded 38,000 flint workings of which 1,000 were finished tools or weapons.

DOWNTON'S DAWN

SCENE: It is a clear bright early summer's day. A girl, clearly pregnant, is sitting on the top of a small hillock looking over the river and the reeds and willow beyond. She is wearing simple leather clothes stitched with sinew. She is weaving willow to make a carrier for her baby, her first, due in a month or two. At the foot of the hill, close to the river bank on a gravel ledge perhaps ten feet above the river, smoke is rising from one of the three crudely thatched huts and an old man is sitting on his haunches knapping flints. Skins are stretched to dry and a woman is scraping one clean.

We hear the girl's thoughts:

'I do hope the hunters find something soon. Last year's nuts and dried crab apples are not enough. We don't seem to catch enough fish although the old man's clever traps are good and my Man is good with a harpoon. I do hope he's safe and looking after my brother on his first hunt. I'm

glad they took the boat - it shows they think there are big animals about. I wonder whether Grandpa is right and we can stay here until after you are born, Baby. This is a safe place - we've been coming here every spring since I was little - but the young men say the game is better now farther north where all the rivers meet. I don't like it there.'

Her mind wanders as she works and then something makes her look up and across the valley. She has known this feeling more strongly since she became fully a woman - an awareness of her kin however far away they are. This time however she can see the flailing arms and then hear the faint cries of her small brother as he comes across the marsh, alone.

'I must warn Granny and Grandpa - perhaps something has gone wrong with the hunters.' So she makes her way awkwardly down to the camp.

"Boy is coming on his own. I do hope they are all right" she says.

"They'll be fine" says Granny without even turning and the Girl gasps because now she can see that Granny is getting ready all the makings of a feast and Grandpa has got out his skins and head-dress and is preparing a thanks offering to the Earth-mother.

'That can only mean that the men have killed a great beast and are on their way back with the meat carried between them hanging from staves. That is always the time for a party. Dare I ask Granny how she knows? And yet didn't I sort of know too?'

"It'll come to you, my love" said Granny before the Girl could speak.....

This story is based on an incident reported by Laurence van der Post while watching the nomadic Kalahari tribesmen who live today much as these early men of Downton may have lived. He drove thirty miles from a kudu kill to find the camp already preparing a kudu feast.

FARMING BEGINS

Around 5,000 years ago permanent settlement, farming and a marked increase in population had occurred in the Avon valley. Rivers were highways for primitive men but, as in the case of the River Avon at Downton, sometimes they became frontiers between tribes as well. The valley and the forested chalk upland behind the river were rich in game, wildfowl and fish.

The names given to prehistoric periods are very arbitrary but here they are taken to be:

PALAEOLITHIC	Old Stone Age	400,000 to 10,000 BC
MESOLITHIC	Middle Stone Age	8,000 to 3,500 BC
NEOLITHIC	New Stone Age	3, 500 to 2,000 BC
BRONZE AGE		2,000 to 800 BC
IRON AGE		800 BC to 43 AD
ROMAN		43 AD to 400 AD
POST-ROMAN		400 AD to 500 AD
SAXON		500 AD to 1066

To the west, just above Downton on New Court Down, are the Giant's Grave, a Neolithic long barrow or burial mound, and the Bronze Age round barrow or tumulus called Giant's Chair. The lynchets of Standlynch are

Iron Age round hut

terraced fields cut out of the side of the hill to improve fertility and could date from this period. These constructions indicate a considerable degree of social organisation and a settled population over thousands of years. Doubtless the villagers were recruited to help build Stonehenge, another massive communal project, only 15 miles to the north.

Quern

By 3,000 BC, Downton men were of the 'Beaker' people, migrants from the Continent. They were ploughing, tending flocks of sheep and had pottery. They probably brought their domesticated stock with them from the mainland of Europe. Their crops were 20% wheat, 80% barley. Their homes were still circular but quite sophisticated compared with the Mesolithic shelters of 4,000 years earlier. They wove and made sophisticated pottery. In Castle Meadow, in much the same area as earlier man had built his shelters, several round Neolithic hut foundations dating from 1,500 BC were discovered.

Bread oven

As well as burying their dead in barrows they may already have set aside for their collective worship the yew covered hillock, close to water, that is now the churchyard. They seem to have felt themselves surrounded by the spirits and very especially that of the Earth-mother. Whenever they were about to dig foundations or a storage or rubbish pit, they first sacrificed some animal as a propitiation. Their burial chambers have an almost womb-like design.

To judge by reports of men like Julius Caesar, who had a first look at Britain in 55 BC, these Celts were very aggressive and very quarrelsome. They would return from battles they had won carrying the heads of the vanquished. Particularly classy heads were preserved and brought out to impress visitors. They were very fond of a good party and their social organisation within each tribe was effective and just. However, their failure to unite above tribal level made it easier for invaders.

Iron Age fort

IRON AGE DETERRENTS

Generally, the hill forts built by the Celts - or British, as they came to be known - were not permanently settled although South Cadbury, Maiden Castle and Danebury certainly were. Many had plentiful storage pits suggesting that, when threatened, grain and other stocks were hoarded and guarded inside the defences.

Clearbury hill fort

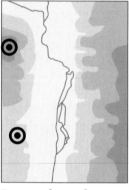

Long and round barrows

At Clearbury, a couple of miles north-west of Downton, the highest hill, now tree covered, was one of these dominating, intimidating earth forts. With its high bank and deep ditch, built in the Iron Age, about 500 years BC, it must have been an excellent deterrent to neighbours thinking of trespass. Clearbury is only just over 2 Hectares in extent so large numbers of people or livestock could not have been protected for any length of time.

A succession of hill top forts on both sides of the river served as boundary markers as well as defensive strong points for the local tribes and, as the sun shone on the bare chalk of their raised and palisaded banks, they would have served as a very visible deterrent to aggressive neighbours. One of the tribes was called Wilsaeta and they gave their name to Wilton. Did their territory extend as far as Clearbury, eight miles from Wilton? Was it they who built the fort?

THE BELGAE RULE DOWNTON.....

Downton - 'the farm (or hamlet) by the hill' (or, perhaps, 'by the water') in the language of the men who first dwelt here in any numbers - had all sorts of advantages for early settlers. Its biggest advantage, however, was its good river ford allowing trade to travel east and west as well as north and south. By 100 BC the tribes living in the Downton area were from a wave of Celts from Northern France called Belgae who had exiled themselves from northern France after their leader quarrelled with the rest of his tribe, partly on how to deal with the Romans.

The hillock that is now called the Moot was well placed to be a strong point to defend the crossing from attack although as yet we have no evidence of such use earlier than Norman times. The crossing itself was hard enough for horses and cattle and perhaps even carts to ford the river.

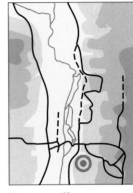

Roman villa

Downton Roman Villa

.....AND THEN THE ROMANS.....

When the Romans came in force in 43 AD under Emperor Claudius some of the Belgae and the neighbouring tribe of Durotriges to the south-west resisted their invasion. In subjugating them, the Roman General, later, Emperor, Vespasian, destroyed 20 of their forts in the south of England. There was a particularly vicious battle at Maiden Castle in Dorchester.

Soon, however, their new British subjects were benefiting from Roman peace and order and resulting trade. More and more the administration passed back to the locals and in the Romano-British Villa, thought to be built before 300 AD, we at last get the remains of a house in Downton that we would recognise today. To people used to round, thatched huts the squared flint walls, tiled roofs, hot water and underfloor heating must have seemed the height of sophistication and luxury.

It was a long building, mostly one room thick. It had 17 or 18 rooms, some giving off each other, and outside, roofed passageways. With its fine tessellated floor (now in Salisbury Museum), bathroom and under-floor heating, it was clearly

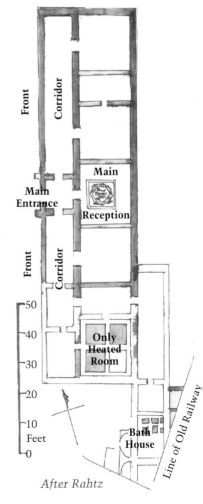

After Rahtz

the home of a wealthy man, probably the local ruler, keen to show off his Roman culture at a time when Roman rule was already less secure but still dominant.

It would probably have been the centre of a country estate geared to producing food for export to Rome and its Empire and to feed the Roman army. We know they harvested at least three kinds of wheat and some barley. About 15% of the crop was a vetch, possibly as a supplementary feed for the cattle that were the most important of the farm animals they reared.

Given the date, the first owner might have been of Romano-British rather than Roman stock. During the 5th Century AD as the Roman power waned, the southern Britons recruited mercenaries from the German tribe of Franks to defend them from marauders from the north and from overseas. Some of the mercenaries lived and were buried at Charlton, a couple of miles upstream from Downton.

LIFE IN THE VILLA

Cast:

Marcus: Aged 35. Big, bluff ex-soldier now enjoying running the great estate and his own farm to supply the army locally and across in France. If only Flavia would cheer up and count her blessings...

Flavia: Just 30, she is slim, dark and neurotic! She does not like living in Britain and feels herself a colonial outcast. She has not yet accepted that she will never see Rome again but it will always be "Home".

Luke: The old family slave. He has been with Flavia since he was given to her when she married. He finds Britain cold but he can endure this - the alternatives for a slave can be worse. He is educated, even cultured.

Olivia and Octavius: 10 and 12. They are Romano-British - their friends are almost all local boys and girls and they find Mummy going on about Rome rather a joke.

Setting: Downton Villa. Coming on the main road from Venta [Winchester] to Sarum [Salisbury], you would have turned off to the left, come along the ridge and then downhill to the ford. Instead of crossing the ford you would have turned left again. As you walked along the river bank you would have found the decaying remains of a Roman fortlet left over from the early days of the occupation and now partly demolished to provide timber for the Villa. The well-rutted lane would take you past the huts and hovels of the estate servants and slaves and then uphill to a fine long, single storey, tiled roof house facing across the valley to the west.

In the centre is a fine room with a handsome tessellated floor and decorated plaster walls. In this room that is warm, but not as warm as Flavia would wish, she is seated. Across the room sitting at a small desk is Luke with pen poised ready to write....

FLAVIA (drawing her shawl round her irritably: **'The Gods help me! If it gets any colder I'll perish ...where was**

I, Luke?'

LUKE: 'You had reached "Dearest Mater..", Madam.'

FLAVIA: 'If someone doesn't get this heating soon this will be my Last Will and Testament... "Dearest Mater"…. at long last the winter seems to be coming to an end…. hah!….The children have had a succession of what these ignorant savages call"…No…Cross that out…

LUKE (innocently): '"The children"? "Ignorant savages"?'

FLAVIA: 'Cross the whole country out as far as I am concerned. Will this winter never end?'

She gets up and crosses to look out of the window. 'Snow, hail and sleet followed by fog, mist and rain… What possessed our revered ancestors to colonise this Gods-forsaken country in the first place?'

LUKE: 'Not my ancestors, Madam'.

FLAVIA: 'No..they had more sense.'

LUKE: 'We have reached… "had a succession of.."'

FLAVIA: "What the British call "colds". Coughs and sneezes all the time. How I long for some of Rome's glorious sunshine!"

LUKE: 'Put that in ?'

FLAVIA: 'Certainly! It's the truest word I've spoken'.

LUKE: 'We don't want to upset the dowager, Madam'.

FLAVIA: 'Oh, all right! Umm.. "if the estate is really successful we may manage to come home for a visit one day…but, for the moment, I must wait impatiently for news of you by the next messenger… if he hasn't frozen to death on the way…"

FLAVIA and LUKE together: 'Don't put that in!'

FLAVIA: "We planted the snowdrop bulbs you sent us two years ago (Ye Gods! Is it that long?!) on the slopes of our fields, down by the river. They have taken to this alien climate very well and this month there has been a wonderful display....."

LUKE: 'Wonderful. A sheet of flowers blossoming like the snow'.

FLAVIA: 'Mmm   I like that... put it in....snow....then put "The children love the snow When it is very cold they build statues out of it.   Mercifully it seldom comes this far south but Marcus tells me he used to see lots of it when he was fighting the barbarians in the north".

Marcus, Octavius and Olivia rush in. They are in great spirits. Flavia's reaction to this heartiness is to draw her shawl a bit tighter around her shoulders....

MARCUS, having kissed Flavia warmly, he offers a mocking bow: 'Greetings, O Flavia, mistress mine...we bring great news.... they've finished the bath house and it will be firing up tonight.'

OCTAVIUS: 'I really like the colours - orange and red is just right for somewhere hot and steamy...'

OLIVIA: '...well, I think these pale green and yellow stripes in here go even better. It looks like the forest in spring time. And they go so well with the patterns on the floor - but you wouldn't have the taste to see that...

OCTAVIUS: 'Oh, you girls...pretty, pretty. Fancy a game, Luke? I'll get the dice.'

FLAVIA: 'Just a moment, darling...I'm dictating a letter to Granny. Marcus, that's lovely about the bathroom but did you remember to get someone to fix the hypocaust flue - this floor is barely warm. I'm sure it's not working properly and I'm cold...'

MARCUS, swinging her out of the chair and spinning her round: 'What you need is a bit more exercise, old thing. We aren't in Rome any more - you have to run around to keep warm'.

FLAVIA, cheering up but pretending to be annoyed: 'Put

me down! (hissing) Not in front of Luke!'

MARCUS: 'He's used to us by now aren't you, Luke'

LUKE, bowing his head slightly : 'Sir ?'

MARCUS: 'You see, quite used to it! What do you think is wrong with the flue ?'

FLAVIA: 'It's not efficient, like these British workmen. Honestly, you would think they had never heard of under-floor heating.'

MARCUS (cheerfully): 'Of course they haven't! Still it isn't complicated - I'll talk to Cadwael tomorrow - he's a good chap'

OCTAVIUS, has set out a gaming board and is rolling the dice: 'Come on, Luke. Best of five, how do you say ? Pater, Mater, can we go to the potteries tomorrow ?'

FLAVIA: 'Luke and I are writing to Granny so you must wait'

OCTAVIUS: 'Oh.....'

FLAVIA, suspiciously: 'And what have you broken this time ?'

OCTAVIUS: 'Ahh...well...my discus sort of slipped...and sort of knocked over a couple of very old beakers..

FLAVIA: 'And they sort of broke ?'

OCTAVIUS, brightly: 'That's right. They were very old ones...'

FLAVIA: 'You're impossible, Octavius. I sometimes think you do it on purpose because you like going to the Forest potteries'

MARCUS: 'Tell her the rest....'

FLAVIA: 'There's more !?'

OLIVIA, cheerfully : 'You're not going to like this !'

16

FLAVIA: 'Not going to like what, Octavius ?'

OCTAVIUS: 'Well, I sort of hadn't quite got around to the new glass'

FLAVIA: 'In the window, Gods preserve us !'

OCTAVIUS: 'It's a bit sort of chipped'

FLAVIA, exploding : 'I don't believe it. I really don't believe it. How could you ?'

OLIVIA : 'Don't get upset, Mater. It is only a bit chipped'

FLAVIA, working herself up : 'Here I am trying to write a cheerful letter to your Grandmother back home so that she won't worry about us all, stuck out here in the back of beyond... (she starts to sniffle in to her handkerchief)... the back of nowhere....and you are destroying the place even before it is built...'

MARCUS, putting his arm around her while the children look uncomfortable and perhaps even a little contrite : 'Flavia ! Cheer up ! Tell your mother all the good news. The estate is doing very well and I manage an area over three leagues long and one league wide. It's good land and we supply the army here and in Gaul. Our home farm is making enough profit so that we might soon be able to come home for a visit but we have a lovely new house with 18 rooms and every modern convenience here. Tell her that, my dear'

FLAVIA, sniffling still : 'I know, I know...'

MARCUS: 'Life is peaceful...'

FLAVIA : 'Yes it is...'

MARCUS : 'When did we last have a raid ? When did we last even hear of one ?'

FLAVIA : 'I can't remember'

MARCUS : 'Exactly. Belgae is a good Canton - write and tell her that. The sun's out ! Just look at that view - the river and the swans and the flowers.'

FLAVIA, blowing her nose : **'You're right. It is very pretty. Perhaps Spring is on the way.'**

She puts her arm round Marcus' waist and the children gather with them looking out of the window.

MARCUS : 'Of course it is. Look how beautiful our land is. Look at our strong healthy children... they don't even remember Rome any more...this is truly our home.'

Apart from the villa already excavated there are also intriguing signs that there may be remains of something like a Roman gatehouse near the Moot but these have not yet been excavated. Some Roman encampment near this valuable ford would have made military sense in the early days of Roman occupation, the peaceful villa coming 200 years later.

AMBROSIUS PLEADS WITH ROME

Ambrosius was a princely Romano-British ruler. He may have been uncle to 'King' Arthur. Half way through the 5th Century he wrote to Rome: *"I beg you to listen to the groans of the Britons for the barbarians drive us into the sea and the sea drives us back to the barbarians."* **Rome did not reply.**

....THEN THE SAXONS

Perhaps these men told their families at home that England was for the taking. By the end of the century armed Saxon invaders had arrived. Some of the pottery found in the Downton Villa was of Saxon manufacture so it was probably still in use as a house after the Saxons arrived although it then fell in to disuse.

The Saxon Chronicle tells of repeated landings of Saxons in our area. Ealdorman Cerdic and his son Cynric, the earliest, having landed at Totton near Southampton in 495AD, then worked their way north and west to the River Avon, defeating the Celtic British King of the land on the east bank of the Avon, Natanleod, in 508.

One tradition has it that Natanleod was buried at Downton near the Moot at Natanbury, a name in use since at least 1798. This may just be a misunderstanding of the suffix 'bury' which has a more usual meaning of 'fortified place,' or, more likely, a romantic naming only one better than 'Dunroamin.' Among other Saxon invaders, Port landed at Portsmouth and Wightgar was given the Isle of Wight.

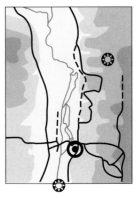

Cerdic's ford?

Saxon battles?

The Moot

In 519, according to one version, the Saxons wanted to push farther westward across the River Avon but found Downton staunchly defended by the British. Cerdic is said to have diverted his army to a ford down river, north of Castle Hill, and won his crossing at what was now to be called Cerdices-ford or, today, Charford. This outflanked defenders of the best ford at Downton who were perhaps relying on the Moot, Clearbury and Witherington hill forts as their fortified strong points, the forts at Castle Hill and Godshill having already fallen to Cerdic. After the battle Cerdic had established the kingdom of the West Saxons and rule over the Avon valley.

Although there is little or no contemporary written evidence to corroborate this story it fits well with the slow build up of Saxon power as more and more immigrants arrived and demanded more and more land up the Avon Valley. On the early Saxon charters one of the boundaries of Downton went from Telegraph Hill to Charford and was called the Warpath.

Cynric fought and won a battle somewhere between Charford and Salisbury and then was victorious at Salisbury in 552. One Victorian map shows Witherington camp as the scene of a battle, other antiquarians thought it was at Downton. Once the Saxons had taken Downton and Salisbury there seems to have been another pause before they continued their Western advance in to Dorset and Devon, splitting the British Celts whom they called Welsh. Some of the Celts were pushed in to Wales and others in to Devon and Cornwall (and Brittany, in France, named after them). They may have been weakened by Plague.

In secure possession of both banks of the river, the mound now called the Moot, would have been less relevant as a defensive position. This may explain the absence of superficial traces of its use as a fort by the Saxons although no substantive excavation has yet been carried out there. Traces of Saxon dwellings have been found in the Castle Meadow area but many more are probably buried beneath our present houses and some cottages may even re-use original Saxon foundations.

WALLIES !

'Wal' from which Wales and Welsh derive had the meaning of 'slave' or 'serf' to the Saxons and the hamlet of Walton, where New Court and Wick now are, was presumably where the existing population were housed and allowed to continue farming after the Saxon conquest.

WAS DOWNTON A SAXON ROYAL STOPOVER?

Less important militarily once the river had been crossed, Downton is thought to have been nevertheless the site of one of a dozen Saxon royal villas in Wiltshire. Its choice as well for one of the early Saxon churches points to Downton having remained an important centre of local government right through the Dark Ages.

Did the Saxon church look like this?

We may never be sure where the royal villa was in Downton but the Saxon Kings liked ready-made moats and often chose islands or places almost surrounded by rivers - Wilton is a good example. If they did that in Downton, what is now an island below the mills (but might then have been on a promontory sticking out from the East bank) could be the place. It only took its present shape when the mill race was cut through to give a straighter flow back in to the river many centuries later.

There are suggestions that at the time when the Moot was fortified the river ran through where the pond now is - this would explain why the bank and ditch were built as they are, not reaching the present water's edge. Whether or not the Saxon villa was on it, the island almost certainly was the site of the Bishop's palace more recently. It came to be called Old Court or King John's Palace.

OLD COURT OR KING JOHN'S PALACE

Little excavation has been carried out on the island below the mills but one trial pit was dug. It suggested that there was indeed a large building there which contained greensand stone blocks, brought perhaps from Chilmark. One small decorated capital [column's top] found was dated as 12th - 13th Century. Old Court went through many changes but seems to have been used last in 1578 by which time it was already very dilapidated. Later references are only to the letting of land for grazing.

With Britford and Wilton, parts of Downton were passed in Saxon royal Wills indicating that these were key elements of the Saxon kingdom not to be handed out to others able to misuse their strategically important positions. It is quite likely that the basic composition of the Downton Hundred and, later, the Parish, dates back to Roman times at least. Downton's Roman villa, then at its heart, served as what might more recently have been called the Manor House. There is far more continuity in our English landscape than is always immediately obvious.

St Birinus

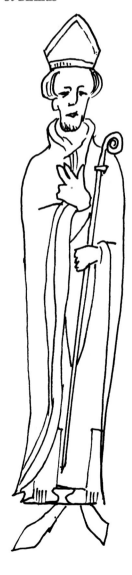

ST BIRINUS COMES TO DOWNTON AND THE SAXON CHURCH IS BUILT

In 638 AD the first Bishop to the West Saxons, St Birinus, came to consecrate a church in Downton. This followed the conversion and baptism of King Cynegils in 635. He had had King Oswald of Northumbria as his sponsor or Godfather. At the same time the Bishop also consecrated another small church where Winchester cathedral now stands.

This was only four years after Birinus, a Roman monk from Northern Italy, had been told by the Bishop of Genoa, by order of Pope Honorius I, to go and sow the seeds of 'our Holy Faith in distant lands beyond the English dominions where no other teacher had been before him.' He was hastily made a Bishop and on landing in Hampshire in 634 he found the West Saxons, comparatively new arrivals in Britain, so completely heathen that he decided to preach the word of God amongst them rather than seek more distant converts in Scotland.

The present dedication of the church in Downton to St Laurence may well go back to St Birinus for whom St Laurence, martyred in the 3rd Century, would have been a familiar and much revered Saint. After consecration as a bishop, St Birinus was based at Dorchester-on-Thames and it was there he died in 650 AD.

ST LAURENCE

Local rumour had it that the church which Laurence led before a period of persecution had been very wealthy. The pagan ruler summoned him and demanded the church's treasure. Laurence said he needed three days to gather it. At the end of the three days he took the ruler to the church and showed him hundreds of poor and sick people there, saying *'These are the riches of our church.' For this he was roasted on a gridiron. He demanded to be turned over 'as that side was done.'....*

He and the other missionary bishops following on from St Augustine, the first Archbishop of Canterbury, took advantage of the custom that each pagan chief selected and financed his own shaman or priest with what we now call tithes. When the rulers converted to Christianity they were 'allowed' to continue this practice by nominating and paying for their own priests. This gave the bishops a funded priesthood who could work closely with the rulers.

Kings in those days needed to keep moving around, making their presence felt and ensuring local Jarls did not get ideas above their station. A characteristic of the more permanent Saxon royal stopping places was that they all had a church close to the royal villa. Downton now also had its royal manor house next to a new church and round it will have gathered and dwelt those who were to run the royal estate, serfs and slaves and tenant farmers.

DOWNTON GIVEN TO THE CHURCH - FROM TIME TO TIME....!

In 648 King Cynwalh gave his manor estate at Downton to the See of Winchester in fulfilment of the dying wish of his father King Cynegils, grandson of Cerdic, and he himself had a new Minster built in Winchester. Although sometimes taken back into royal hands, perhaps to provide land for some of their thegns (thanes), and perhaps because the Kings had temporarily reverted to paganism, later Kings reaffirmed the gift of Downton to the church.

From 860 the West Saxon capital was in Sherborne because the Vikings/Danes had seized and burnt Winchester. King Alfred, a descendant of Cerdic, finally defeated them in 878 and returned the capital to Winchester.

In 997, when Downton was once again and finally returned to them by King Ethelred, the Bishop's estate was divided. Downton was one unit, down from 100 mansae to 55 with Bishopstone taking the other 45. [Mansae seems to be the monks' bookish Latin for tithings or what we might today call holdings or farm tenancies. It derives from the Latin for dwelling. In this area it may equate to Hide as the Bishop held 60 Hides 100 years later.] Various bits had been alienated or chopped off. King Canute (1016-35) took Witherington and Standlynch out of the Bishop's portion. By Domesday, in 1086, Redlynch, Hamptworth, Woodfalls and Charlton were all hived off. The Bishop's estate was assessed at not quite 60 hides - still a substantial holding of perhaps 7,000 acres.

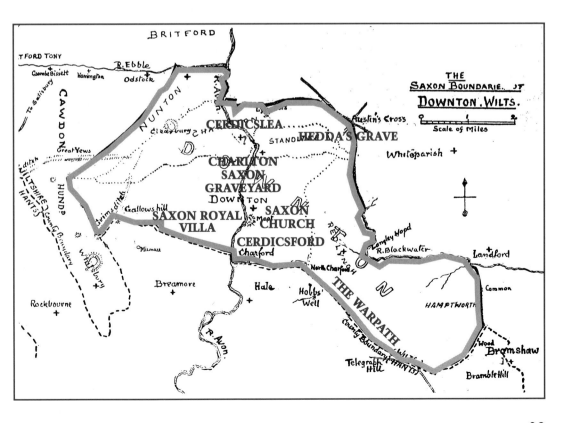

PEPPERBOX HILL AND HEDDA

The fifth Bishop of the West Saxons, and the first to be based at Winchester, was Hedda. He probably died in 705 on the estate at Downton which for many years afterwards included Haeddi's Grove at Pepperbox Hill. He was said to be buried up there and his grave is mentioned in the description of the boundaries of Downton in early Saxon charters. The Venerable Bede says 'many miraculous cures have been wrought in the place where he died through the merit of his sanctity.' Hedda had had the remains of St Birinus transferred to the cathedral in Winchester where one may see his sarcophagus and also the chests containing the bones of the early Saxon Kings.

MONKISH FORGERY?

There are scholars who use the fact that some of the documents referring to Downton, St Birinus and the Kings date from some hundreds of years later than the events they record to cast doubt on the stories themselves. In some cases the original records had been destroyed in Viking raids and monks were setting down their memory of what was in them. Although there was a power struggle between the Sees of Winchester and Salisbury, it is hard to see how the scribes could have totally falsified the story even if they embroidered it. Oral tradition was still very important and their contemporaries would soon have complained of wilful invention. There were a number of corroborative documents from successive Saxon Kings still in existence, then and even now, to show that Downton had been given to the Bishops of Winchester even if sometimes taken back for a time.

SAXON FARMERS

Saxon plough

The farming of the second half of the first millennium in Downton was similar to that practised by the Saxons in Germany. Individual plots, common tillage and common pasture required a degree of social organisation that had resulted in the development of the moot or village gathering to plan communal activity and settle disputes. To some extent this would have applied even on a royal estate. Clear direction at the top would be needed to manage the annual migration of sheep up on to the downs for summer grazing, the ploughing, sowing and harvesting of arable land in the valleys, the beginning of planned drainage of the marshes and the rearing of cattle, goats and pigs. Forest clearance both provided timber for housing an expanding population and also more grazing.

Saxon hut

DUNTONE
DOWNTONE
DUNTON
DUNTONA
DONTONA
DOWNTON
DUNCTON
DUNCKTON
DONKETON
DANE-KNUT-TUN
DEAN-NUK-TUN

DOWNTON, DOUNTONE, DUNTON, DUNCTON, DONKETON, DUNTONE.....

Spelling was never too important to our ancestors. The derivation of the name of the village is not known but one widely accepted and simple explanation is that it comes from the Saxon words dun or down for a hillock and ton or tun for a farm or hamlet. Tuns were, however, often named after their owner and we know that the le Dune or Dun family still held land at Witherington only a couple of miles north of Downton in 1089. One very imaginative 18th Century version offers Dane-knut-tun or Dean-nuk-tun!

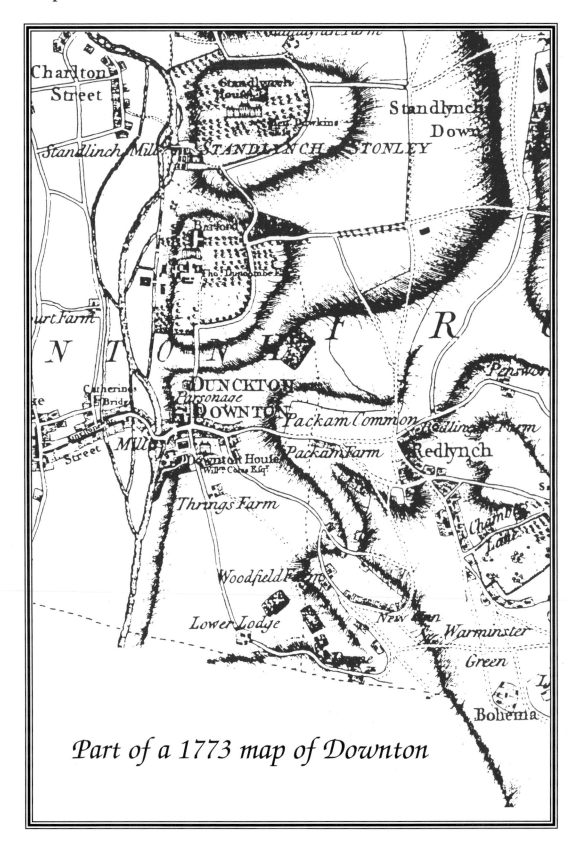

Part of a 1773 map of Downton

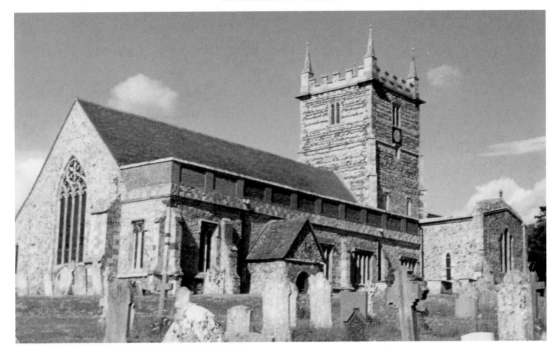

Downton - *the 'village on a hill'* - is in two parts.

The original settlement grew on the ridge above the river (on the left as one looks at the bridge.) The Borough, created in 1209, runs across the valley to right and left of the bridge.

River Avon, Catherine (or Iron Bridge) and Creel Cottage looking south

High Street

The Borough, Downton Cross and the White Horse

The Borough

Witherington Farm, Longford Castle with the River Avon in flood

The Mills and Tannery

Moot House

South Lane Baptist Church

Borough Cross

Chapter 2

The Normans Shape Downton

NORMAN INVASION: NEW BISHOPS - NEW CHURCH

By the time of the Norman conquest in 1066, Downton was a long-established community, a centre of one of many large land holdings owned by the Bishop of Winchester, given to him or confirmed by successive Saxon Kings.

It gave its name to a Hundred stretching 11 miles from No Man's Land to Nunton. One can still see from the top of the hill at Clearbury the typical land division, known as tithings or hides, which divided the land in strips running from the river straight up to the ridge behind so that each tenant got some of the marshy fertile valley land and some of the drier less fertile but valuable hill pasture.

A HUNDRED HIDES

A Hundred has various descriptions but one of the most useful is that it was divided up in to 100 Hides, each Hide or tithing being enough land to support a farmer and his family and servants - commonly about 125 acres. Downton still had 100 hides before the Conquest but not by the time of the Domesday survey.

The Bishop's estate was becoming ever more focused on arable farming. Sheep were very important not only for their wool and meat but also to fertilise the corn-lands; the lighter the land the more sheep were kept for this purpose. Eventually this was to rob the hill tops of fertility so that they were of little use until the invention of chemical fertilisers.

Downton was affected by the creation of the King's New Forest south and east of the village. It was said to have lost 2 Hides - say, 250 acres - to the new inclosure. Quite likely William the Conqueror's visit to Downton was to establish the limits of his new hunting areas.

The fanatical pursuit of hunting by the Norman Kings who had built Clarendon Palace as a hunting lodge for Melchett Forest, just up the road from Downton, may well have been of profit to the Bishop's estate. When the Court was at Clarendon supplies were sometimes bought from Downton and the Court was often there.

SAXONS SUPPLANTED BY NORMANS

The Saxon Church in England had gone through a reinvigorating upheaval in the century before the Normans came. St Dunstan, born in Somerset, Abbot of Glastonbury and then Archbishop of Canterbury for 18 years, brought a new discipline, vitality and scholarship which showed in a great upsurge of ecclesiastical art and music as well as some fine new churches and cathedrals.

The Normans recognised the importance of this by rapidly imposing a new ecclesiastic hierarchy and building many Norman-style churches and cathedrals.

William the Conqueror was a toughie, determined to control his ever larger kingdom. He feared the Church. His seizure of England had been grudgingly accepted by the Pope but there were plenty of other rulers seeking the Pope's ear to get him to change his mind. William would not accept the Pope's authority in such matters and ordered the Bishops not to correspond with the Pope.

One of the Normans' most political acts was to build a new cathedral in Winchester, starting in 1079. They then knocked down its fine Saxon predecessor, the centre of the Saxon religious revival, which had only finished a refurbishment, started by King Alfred's son Edward, in 994.

In 1086, as part of the Norman reorganisation of the church and probably partly to decrease the power of the Diocese of Winchester, the Bishop of Sherborne was transferred to Old Sarum. He continued to oversee the Diocese of Ramsbury. Downton then became part of the Salisbury Diocese although mostly still owned by the Bishop of Winchester. To acknowledge the Bishop of Salisbury's authority the rectory of Downton paid half a mark (17 pence) annually to the Bishop of Salisbury. These days it is still paid by Winchester College but to the Church Commissioners until, and if, it is finally commuted!

William the Conqueror

The Normans had already refortified the old hill fort at Sarum and a new cathedral was built there by Bishop Osmund. His successor, Roger, who was also Henry I's chief minister, managed to get control of the castle and soon had enlarged his cathedral and extended the outer defences of the castle to enclose it.

ECCLESIASTIC POLITICKING?

We know from Domesday in 1086 that there was still a church in Downton four hundred years after St Birinus had consecrated it. Downton was the largest manorial estate in Wiltshire.

Downton entry in Domesday

Although belonging to the Bishop of Winchester it now had its diocesan bishop seven miles up the road. It may help us to understand some of the events of the next two or three hundred years in Downton if we think of it as once again a frontier town but this time a politico-ecclesiastical frontier rather than between tribes.

The entries in Domesday show that the Bishop of Winchester had lost 3 of Downton's 100 Hides in the time of King Canute and the church had lost a further 2. The Bishop was paying taxes on 97 Hides at the time of the Conquest.

Who had acquired the sequestered Hides is not clear. It may have been Waleran the Hunter who had a hide at Standlynch [Staninges] and Edward, who held Witherington [Widetone]

Edward is referred to as a King's thegn and evidently was not the powerful Edward of Salisbury whose grandson, Patrick, was to capture Downton's castle sixty years later. Waleran had extensive holdings farther north and east. Edward is an English name and it is noted that his father had held Witherington before the Normans came.

The Bishop held 7 mills, pasture 6 miles long and 3 miles wide and woodland 5 miles by $1^1/_2$ miles. Three quarters of the land seems to have been tenanted with the other quarter under the church's direct control (demesne.)

DOMESDAY BOOK

Originally called the Roll of Winchester it was indeed a roll of parchment listing holdings and what they were worth in men and agricultural yield so that taxes and calls for military manpower could be more easily assessed.

STEPHEN AND MATILDA

In the early 12th Century there was civil war between the supporters of King Stephen and those of Henry I's only legitimate surviving child, Matilda. Bishop Roger, having been Henry's chief Minister, was on the side of Matilda. He held castles in her interest at Salisbury, Malmesbury, Sherborne and Devizes.

Bishop Henry of Blois in Winchester was Stephen's brother. In 1138 Henry built or strengthened castles at Downton (almost certainly the Moot, perhaps refortified, and almost certainly only a temporary timber structure as there is no evidence of stone walls), Taunton (where he had huge estates), Farnham, Waltham and Merdon.

The palisades go up ...

In 1147 the enterprising Count Patrick seized Downton Castle *'out of the authority and possession of the church of Winchester'* notionally on Matilda's behalf but mainly for the plentiful loot. Count Patrick was nominally Earl of Salisbury as Empress Matilda had ennobled him when she landed at Arundel. Although his grandfather had picked the right side in 1066 and kept his lands one must suspect that Patrick soon found himself out in the wilderness. Today

DOWNTON MOONRAKERS

Another myth attributes to Downton the Moonraker story. King John and his Court made so many visits to Downton, so a contemporary poem tells us, that the villagers refused to support his retinue. The King was cross so he sent knights to punish them. When his delegation arrived they found the peasants up to all sorts of crazy antics including the famous raking of a pond to capture the moon's reflection and trying to drown an eel. King John laughed so much that he forgave them .... or so the story goes! The people of Gotham seem to have first claim to this story but it was undoubtedly expensive to have royal visitors wherever you lived. Later the story transferred to Dorset smugglers accosted by the Revenue!

the *Marquess* of Salisbury is a Cecil and the title dates back only to Elizabethan times.

Matilda had all but given up her claim to the Crown of England by the time Downton was captured by Patrick and she retired to France the following year. After a siege, Downton was soon back in the hands of the Bishop of Winchester as King Stephen consolidated his power.

By 1208 Peter de Roches was Bishop of Winchester and so owner of much of Downton. He had no castle at Downton any more as it had been knocked down after the civil war. He was a strong supporter of King John and later became chief Minister to Henry III.

John visited the Bishop in Downton three times and probably stayed with him in the Bishop's Palace which may have been refurbished at that time. We are not sure where the Palace was but currently the island opposite the Moot and below the mills finds most favour. It may have been about this time that it was made an island to improve the mill race.

King Stephen

THE BISHOP'S COURT

There has been much myth muddling over the years. Some of it comes perhaps from confusion of the legislative Court or Leet with the actual Palace where the Bishop stayed and the Court would sometimes have been held. The Court appears to have moved from Old Court (the Bishop's Palace) to the Borough, somewhere near the cross and the White Horse and then, in mid-14th Century, for a time, to New Court.

It seems that the last time the Bishop actually held his own Court in Downton was in 1571 by which time Old Court was dilapidated if not a ruin. From the 18th Century until the beginning of the 20th Century the Courts were held in Court House, South Lane, which straddles the border between Borough and Manor. One of the Court's main jobs to the end was to sort out wrangles over inheritance and tenancies.

1135 AD: THE DOWNTON CHURCH REBUILT

Now we must turn back to the church itself. As we have seen, Downton had a special place in the hearts of the early West Saxon kings perhaps because the battles for its control were such important steps in establishing the whole kingdom of Wessex. It was the site of a royal home and then of the bishops to whom it must also have been important as they built and stayed often in their palace there.

We can I think safely assume that if stone churches were being built by the Saxons at Britford and Breamore the original, possibly wooden, church consecrated in Downton by St Birinus, the loved and trusted guide to the newly converted Kings and people, would also have been rebuilt in stone. The north transept is out of line with the rest of the present church and the spacing of the pillars in the nave is uneven suggesting use of earlier foundations or a melding of old and new. Master masons favoured old foundations because they knew that they had carried loads for many years and had finished settling.

West Aisle and Nave

That none of that stone church can still be identified except, so the experts say, in the general layout of the church, is perhaps a measure of how important the church already was rather than any idea that only an old and dilapidated wooden chapel was being replaced in 1135. It is mentioned in Domesday.

The earliest visible part of the church, the west end of the nave, is dated between 1130 and 1150 and that coincides with the fortification in the village. It fits well with what we know of Bishop Henry of Blois' other work at this time, notably at St Cross, Winchester. The three western bays of the nave have pointed arches linking Norman or Transitional pillars with simple, slightly amateurish, carved decoration of their capitals. It is of note that the very first pointed arches in England had only been built a few years before. Perhaps the rebuilding of the church was the innovative Bishop's personal project along with the palisades at the Moot and refurbishment of his Downton Palace.

The three new bays of the nave could have been a modern extension to the original Saxon cruciform church. If so, the builders were soon encroaching on the old works as they put in a further two bays with taller pillars and arches. It is the positioning and spacing of these which suggests that they replace something rather than that they were begun from scratch. One has, moreover, to explain the fact that there are clear signs that the third pillars butted on to an end wall before the next two arches were constructed to link with the crossing.

DOWNTON 'NEW TOWN' - THE BOROUGH

When in 1209 Bishop Peter de Roches began his new town or Borough in Downton he was asserting his worldly authority very visibly. By building new towns at Downton, Dinton and Stockbridge with their mills and markets in, or on the border of, the See of Salisbury he was challenging a powerful although junior neighbour.

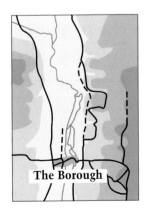

The Borough

When Bishop Peter created the Borough in Downton he did it by letting building plots in 'Free Burgage Tenure' with enough back land to support a family in vegetables.

Gradually these houses became occupied by tradesmen. By 1215 we find a fulling mill for finishing cloth (one of the first in Wiltshire) as well as a corn mill, a tannery, shoemakers, two weavers, several blacksmiths, a wheelwright and basket makers. The fulling mill paid forty shillings rent - £2 in the money of those days, worth so much more today. By 1230 there were 120 tenancies but they never increased beyond 127.

BURGAGE VOTING RIGHTS

Each tenant paid the Bishop of Winchester one shilling a year and their 'Burghage' gave them voting rights. These had only local importance until around 1265 when the first Parliament was summoned to which Downton sent two Burgesses - which it would continue to do until the Reform Act of 1832!

The Bishop also started up a market and Downton might well have grown further but that, ten years later, the construction of Salisbury was started. It soon became the commercial centre for the area.

Neither Downton nor Wilton, important Saxon centres, were ever again to challenge Salisbury. Fifty years later the Bishop of Winchester might even so still have been well satisfied with Peter de Roche's decision. Partly this was luck - the 13th Century had marvellous weather - but it was also good management. In 1264 his great manor, stretching 11 miles from No Man's Land in the South to Nunton in the North, had produced £110 pounds from 677 acres of arable, 100 cattle and 1,700 sheep. For no effort at all the Borough produced another £9 in burgage rents and the profits from the markets. To get a feel for present day values one needs to multiply these figures by between 5 and 10,000!

In England we have relatively few of these 'new towns' but all over South West France one can see the Bastides that were their inspiration. 130 of them were built by their Norman-English overlords to increase commerce. Many of them have grown little and are still functioning as small market towns today much as they and Downton did 750 years ago.

ANCIENT COINS IN THE BOROUGH

The establishment of the Borough all seems so long ago. Only fifty years ago, however, some work in an outhouse at Leicester House in the centre of the Borough uncovered an old wattle and daub wall [a woven frame of sticks covered with plaster left to dry] with pictures of animals scratched in to the surface while it had still been wet. Tucked in to a little hollow in the wall was a small cloth bag that contained coins minted for King Edward I who died in 1307. There were two even older coins from the 12th and early 13th Century, over 100 years earlier. In 1301 William Leicester was one of two Downton Burgesses to represent Downton in that year's Parliament - one of its earliest MPs. Perhaps he hid them before setting off for London?

THE CHURCH EXTENDED

Bishop Peter was also a spiritual authority and under his leadership the church in Downton was reshaped yet again. As we have seen, the nave and aisles were continued for a further two bays and this was done at about the same time as the new town was being created. The junction at the third pair of pillars is very clear.

That was not the end of it. Work continued in the middle of the century when the crossing arches and transepts were built or rebuilt, probably, at least in part, also on old foundations. Finally the chancel was started ca.1275 with provision being made for a tower (dated before the end of the 13th Century) over the crossing. The chancel seems to have been built in two phases and completed by 1320. It is of a markedly higher standard than the rest of the church, probably because this part of the church was for the Bishop. The flint work on the outside is of a very high standard and there are many fine details.

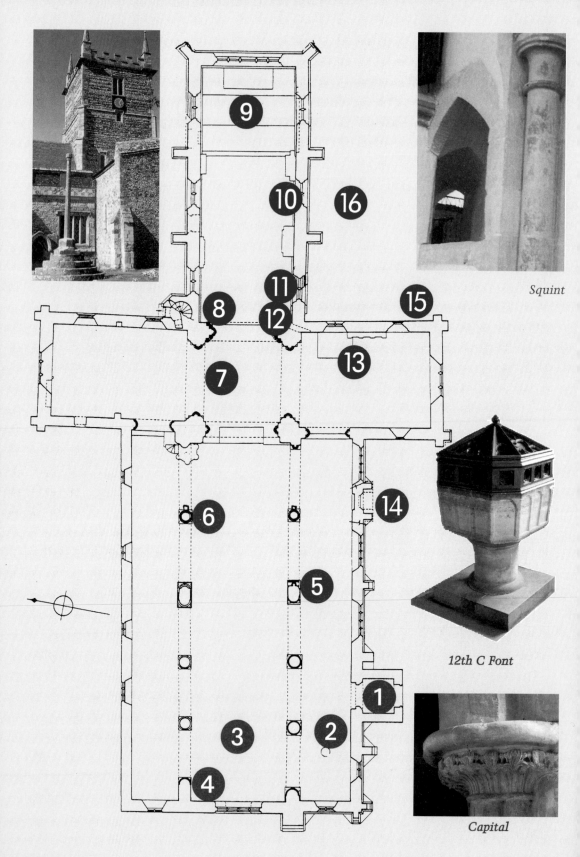

Squint

12th C Font

Capital

A LOOK AROUND ST LAURENCE

The first church was consecrated by St Birinus in 638 but few signs of it remain except in the misalignment of nave and transepts.

1. The porch is dated 1648 which is when the South aisle was rebuilt. The arch and door into the church are 14th Century.

2. The font is of Purbeck marble and was probably made in the 12th Century.

3. The first three arches of the nave are the earliest visible parts of the church and date from 1130AD.

4. Faint traces of a mediaeval wall painting, possibly of Mary riding an ass on the Flight to Egypt, can be seen below the right edge of the West window. The church would have been covered with such story-telling pictures to help illiterate peasants find faith.

5. The third pillars were part of an earlier end wall and the next two, higher, arches were built 50-60 years after the first three.

6. Just above the caps to the fourth pillars there are corbels to carry the Rood beam. The Rood was a larger-than-life wooden carving of the Crucifixion, usually brightly coloured. After the Reformation they were thought idolatrous and removed.

7. Above the Crossing is the belfry and tower. There is a ring of 8 bells and a Sanctus bell which is believed to date from 1400. The earliest of the change rung bells is ca.1450 and the two most recent, 1946, cast as a memorial to those who died in the Second World War.

8. The chancel is the last part of the church to be built, in about 1350. It was probably the private chapel of the Bishop of Winchester who had a Palace on an island below the mills.

9. The Reredos behind the altar shows Christ with the two disciples at Emmaus. St Laurence endured a Victorian restoration in 1860 which saved the tower from collapse but not much else. The East window is entirely Victorian except its sustaining arch.

10. Later the chancel became the private chapel of the Duncombe family whose memorials can be seen.

11. The wooden door below the window was to allow lepers to take Communion.

12. Next to it is a Priest's Squint - a hole through the pillar to allow a second priest in the Lady Chapel to see the priest at the main altar.

13. Sir Charles Duncombe had been a rich goldsmith and Lord Mayor of London. He bought Downton so that he could be its Member of Parliament.

14. Outside, a number of blocked doorways can be seen showing the changes in church usage over the centuries.

15. High on the outside wall of the chancel is a memorial to a faithful servant and in the graveyard, among the many whose families are still in Downton, is the grave of a Flemish evacuee from Flanders in the First World War.

16. Do admire the craftsmanship of the flint masons; it is among the finest in England.

BUILDING FUNDS

Who paid to rebuild the church? A usual pattern in the Middle Ages would have been for the parishioners themselves to pay most.

This was a time of growing population and prosperity but also of political uncertainty. The Church was the outward sign of an inward peace and security that ordinary men and women sought. We find it hard today to realise the insecurity of ordinary men and women who owned little, had no control over weather or pestilence and were constantly finding themselves drawn in to the wars and political upheavals of a very unsettled time.

Their belief in their need for intercessors on their behalf was very deep. Not only were they willing to pay with money and labour for their own church to be built but many of them were to go on the great Crusades or help supply and fund them. In 1334 Downton was paying more tax than any other non-urban place in Wiltshire and the quality and scale of its church building partly reflects that wealth.

Christianity was profoundly important to them. It is no accident that the new church seems to have been built alongside the old, only replacing it once the new work was complete enough for no break in worship. St Birinus' church may well itself have been put on a pagan site of great antiquity - missionary priests presented their ideas as fulfilling all that was best in the old ways. Pope Gregory told them to *'Knock down the idols, not the temples.'*

As both Bishop Henry and Bishop Peter saw Downton in political as well as economic terms, they would probably have partly funded the building themselves so that we have a much larger church than one would expect in a place that in 1377 had only 733 Poll Tax payers. Certainly, there is evidence in the quality of design and workmanship that they supervised what was done here.

Over at least three centuries the Bishops of Winchester maintained a Palace in Downton and the chancel would have been his chapel within the church. There was a separating wall or partition with a door between the chancel and the rest of the church that was not demolished until 1860. The stone altar in those early days was in the crossing, not at the end of the chancel as it is today. The Bishop would have had a private chapel in his Palace as well, as did the resident chaplain in what is now Parsonage Manor but was the Minster until about 1340.

CHURCH FASHIONS

The Norman bishops had by 1350 completely replaced the Saxon church with one after their own taste. The church

12th and 13th C Arches - note end wall remains on right hand pillar

would however go through many more changes in fashion over the centuries that followed as the Renaissance reached across Europe.

Probably any of the vigorous early English carving characteristic of Saxon churches and still to be seen at the surviving Saxon church at Breamore would have been destroyed in the Downton rebuild by the Normans who had a different artistic vision. There would however have been fine carving of stone and wood in the new church and the walls would have been covered with murals of different biblical scenes. There would have been statues of saints, stained glass windows and much else to bring to life the stories read to the largely illiterate congregation Sunday by Sunday.

A great Rood Screen near the end of the nave with a graphic and massive wooden sculpture of the crucifixion, painted in vivid colour, would have stretched up towards the roof and dominated their worship. The corbels on which this probably rested can be seen on the last pillars before the crossing.

Pews would have been introduced and, sadly, soon there would have been a rental charge for sitting in them. You paid more if you were close to the pulpit, less at the back.

Today, after the fury of the Reformation and the Commonwealth, almost all we have left from mediaeval times is one faded mural painting of a donkey, the corbels or supports that may have carried the Rood screen beam, a reinstated glass window brought from elsewhere, the beautiful great oak door made in the 14th Century and a fine font made of Purbeck stone about 1200. Even the font has been much altered over the generations but we do have, still, the lovely church itself to remind us of the commitment of those men and women of 800 years ago.

Chapter 3

A Busy Little Town

CROSSING OF THE WAYS: DOWNTON A HUB

The lines of the old roads converging on Downton are still clearly visible. Some of them are still in use as roads, more of them are now just footpaths and a few can only be seen as the line of a hedge. Those roads are what made Downton.

Wick Lane from over the downs to the west is the clearest, heading east and down Long Close until it disappears in line with the back boundaries of the Borough plots. The land to the north, Catherine Mead, was turned in to water-meadows in the 17th Century and the continuation of Long Close is now a ditch rather than a lane.

The Old Roads

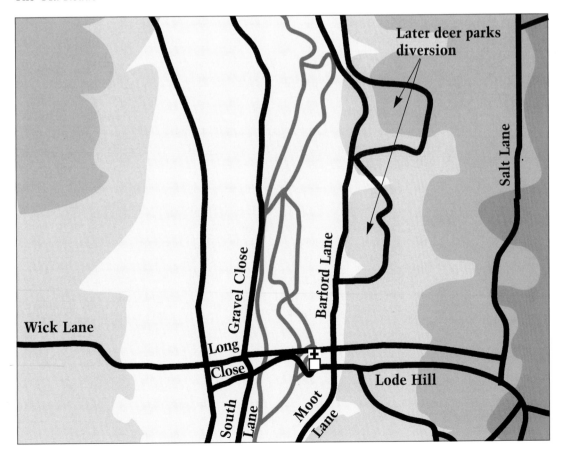

Mill Pool

The ford to which it led seems to have been somewhere below the church or the manor, upstream of Catherine Bridge. Wild Weir, farther upstream from the bridge, was raised in height to give a greater head of water to the mills. That, together with the construction of the water-meadows, makes it impossible to be sure now where the drovers used to cross with their cattle. There are some signs and a local tradition that there was a ford just below the cottages below the bridge.

Logic suggests that the line of the Borough was chosen to lead traffic to the new bridges across the Avon which seem to have been built or improved at the same time as the Borough together with the mill leets and races for the mills. All helped make Downton a new commercial centre. Catherine's Bridge, now called Iron Bridge, has been rebuilt at least three times since.

These changes would have made the ford less important although perhaps still used by the ox drovers coming down Wick Lane on their way east to London. This was part of the Weymouth to London 'main' road that came through Martin and joined with Ox Drove on Wick Down before dropping to the Avon valley and Downton.

Having crossed at the ford, the Wick Lane through-route may originally have run up the churchyard wall past the Parsonage Manor up Doctor's Alley and then up the hill till it forked on the ridge above. A 19th Century map shows the old lane still cutting through the new railway station and continuing up the hill. There are those still living who remember riding horses up it. One can assume that by the 19th Century it was already less used. By 1837 the present High Street/ Lode Hill road route was well established.

At the top of the hill the old road met Salt Lane, now Muddyford Road, which was possibly then the main east-west route which went along Barford Down and Pepperbox Hill. Another road went through Lover and a third went along the Ridge. Lode Hill cutting was deepened to allow the new railway line to pass over it.

Doctor's Alley today

In early times, before the Borough was developed, the main road to Salisbury would likely have been Barford Lane (rather than Gravel Close on the west side of the river) which ran much more directly along the east bank of the river than it now does. In 1385 it is referred to as the 'common King's Highway.' The diversions of Barford Lane round Barford Park and Standlynch House, later Trafalgar House, are evidence of gentrification in the 17th and 18th Centuries when the landowners created their own enclosed deer parks and forced the peasantry to go round.

Marker stones are found in the area and are often what in the local dialect were called 'sarsens.' Typically they are large, long sandstone or heathstone blocks, well rounded by abrasion. They may be what geologists call 'erratics' left by Ice Ages miles from their original homes - not by the last Ice Age, of course, as that did not reach this far south.

There is one such sarsen by the Borough Cross known as the Whipping Stone. Both this stone and a smaller one for long beside Barford Lane seem to have been used to mark the old roads and boundaries.

What was probably initially a secondary road to Salisbury followed the line of South Lane and Gravel Close past New Court to Charlton. It was eventually upgraded to bring coaches in to the centre of the village and then in turn lost status when the north/south road through Wick and the headlands was built in the 18th Century, probably around 1720 which is the date of 'The Bull' public house.

The Headlands and
'The Bull'

TRAVELLERS' REST

The Bull was relatively late in providing travellers with places to eat, drink and sleep in Downton. We know of a 'hostel' in the town in 1503. The White Horse (which was probably that hostel) is mentioned by name in 1599. It was also probably the inn sufficiently well established by 1576 to be persuading the justices not to allow rivals to trade in competition with it. A great mushrooming of hostelries and bars occurred at this time and both wine making and brewing were well established.

The 'White Horse'

The earliest parts of what is now known as the Manor House but ought perhaps more properly be known as the Rectory or Parsonage Manor, next to the Church, may have been built as early as 850 AD to house the five clergy who ministered to the people of Downton. They may also have run the Bishop's estate until this was taken over by lay bailiffs. It would very likely have taken in passers-by as did the larger religious establishments.

13TH CENTURY ECONOMICS

The Bishop of Winchester was a great feudal lord and by Norman times he was running his many estates just as commercially as his lay rivals.

On the appointment of the first Rector, William de Hamilton, in 1281, Downton ceased to have a Minster or Parsonage with a group ministry and bailiffs running the demesne lands (the ones not rented out). To be a Rector of a huge parish like Downton was to be a wealthy man. Rectors appointed curates or parish chaplains to do the pastoral work and often lived away. When we next hear of the Parsonage Manor it is referred to both as the Rectory and as the home of the Parish Chaplain. William de Hamilton had moved on within 5 years to become the King's Vice-Chancellor.

In 1208 there had been 838 acres of demesne [land directly managed by the church] given over to arable. These fields would have been worked either by tenants (villeins and bordars) who owed labour as well as produce to their lord as rental for their tithing or small farm or by serfs who were landless servants tied to the manor for housing and food in exchange for their service. Much of the area would have been one great open field worked in narrow strips. These now belonged to the Parsonage Manor which funded the Rectorship that also took the Great Tithes for the whole parish.

The Bishop's estate may by this time have been managed from New Court which was first built around 1218. It is assumed that Old Court, now on an island, slowly fell into disuse. It is likely that the channel cutting it off from the Moot was part of the work done to build the mills for Bishop Peter de Roche's new town. In 1647 Old Court was still there but valued only for its materials and pasture. On an 18th Century map a sketch of impressive ruins shows it was still not demolished by then.

STRANGE VICAR

Only nine years after William de Hamilton, the first Rector, had been installed by the King, Downton had one of its strangest incumbents. He was called William Burnell. He was 21, nephew of Edward I's Chancellor. He had not even been ordained a priest, and had been given special dispensation by the Pope to be Vicar of Downton even although he held other benefices.

Hold other benefices he certainly did as he was Provost of Wells, held prebends [salaried posts] in York, Lincoln and Salisbury and had been licensed to live away from Downton 'to study.' The Bishop of Salisbury challenged his appointment but it was confirmed by the Pope.

In 1292, with his uncle Bishop of Bath and Wells, he was elected Dean of Wells and by a dispensation from his uncle was able also to remain Provost of Wells and Rector of Downton but only until it was declared a breach of canon law. As soon as Burnell was elected Dean of Wells the Bishop of Winchester nominated his Clerk, Robert of Maidstone, as Rector on the grounds that Burnell couldn't be in two places at once. The outcome of a long wrangle seems to have been that Robert de Harwedon took Burnell's place in 1304. He was a Royal Justice and Keeper of the Bishopric in Winchester where he may well have remained. Burnell was not quite done with Downton as he endowed a Chantry Priest to say prayers for his soul in Downton. The Priest's home was Vine Cottage on Lode Hill near the Slab Lane turning.

THE CHURCH AND ITS TENANTS

It is easy to say that the parishioners paid for the building of their church but how did they earn the money?

The tenants were able to sell produce, cattle and sheep. Slowly the Church and great landowners moved over to a straight money rental rather than taking in kind or labour. This forced the tenants to increase production.

By 1347 the demesne arable acreage in the bishop's estate in Downton was down to 300 and in the next century to 200. The fact was that the great expansion of corn growing to match the increase in population was too much for the land. So much so that by 1250 the average smallholding was reduced to 2 acres as the landowners and farmers inclosed more and more common land. One third of the men were landless. If the harvest failed many starved.

Desperate measures were taken. Strip lynchets were cut in to hill sides to provide extra acreage although only occasional and slight traces are visible in Downton. A terrible harvest in 1315 showed how marginal the farming economy had become. The price of corn trebled and death rates increased by 10%. This was just the worst of many bad years - it has been called a mini-Ice Age with rain and snow seemingly unceasing for years on end.

Despite this the population in the Avon valley grew steadily right up to the Black Death that swept England in 1349 and 1361.

Through this time the Bishops of Winchester were letting out more and more of their demesne land as individual farms or whole manors in an attempt to maintain revenue, preferring rental to running their own estates. It was the mediaeval equivalent of privatisation in what we would call a recession if not a depression.

WINCHESTER COLLEGE TAKES OVER

In 1380, with the King's blessing, Bishop William of Wykeham made over 5 hides of demesne land attaching to St Laurence church (which ran from the north side of High Street up to Barford) to his newly founded Winchester

College together with the advowson or right of appointment of the Rector or Vicar. He also made over the tithes for the whole parish - more than 30 square miles of it - yielding 10% of all its produce - to support the college.

The College, having started with just 70 *'poor and needy scholars,'* and now perhaps the premier, certainly the best, Public School in England, still has the right of appointment of the Vicar of St Laurence, Downton. It still pays 17 pence every year to the Church Commissioners in acknowledgment that Downton is in the See of Salisbury! In its early days it was expected to reserve 10 places for poor boys from Downton from which it derived so much of its income.

Parsonage Manor

Perhaps the switch of Downton lands to the new College, which had been set up partly to train replacement clergy, coincided with an unfilled and unfillable vacancy here. In 1383 Nicholas de Alresford was appointed as the Rector. In 1385 he became the first Vicar, the College taking over the Rectorship. The new Vicar needed a vicarage and so the house where the 'parish chaplain' had lived - Parsonage Manor - was given more land and the Bishop paid out of his own money for the house to be improved. The land ran up to the 'common King's Highway' to the east - Barford Lane - and took a sizeable portion out of other church land.

There is reference to *'these new buildings of stone walls with tiles roofing, greater and lesser, with stone fireplaces, which formerly were the chief rooms of the Rector of the same church which is in the lower part of the property of the Rector with the oratory attached, built strongly of stones and supported by cement, divided into three rooms by stone walls.'* There was a separate kitchen and the northern end was a chapel.

LIFE IN 14C DOWNTON

We know all too little about how people lived in Downton then but we get clues from Wills and from Poor House records. The Wills show that even a Yeoman with his own rented farm of perhaps 120 acres (one hide) would count most of his wealth in his livestock.

He might have a table, a bench, a chair and a very few cooking pots. He would probably have had only one thick cloak. There would be only one bedroom and often only one enormous bed for all the family. One hearth, often with no chimney, and its use not encouraged because timber on the chalk lands was scarce.

Bread would be baked in a communal oven in the village. He would have bread and beer or soup for breakfast. Meat of some kind for three meals a week and bread and cheese on the others. He and his family would go to Church twice on a Sunday.

WYCLIF AND THE LOLLARDS

Sadly, the good times before the plague were too good to last in other ways as well. The clergy had become soft and corrupt as well as the people and it took a John Wyclif to bring a challenge to new spiritual life. He attacked the Church's corruption. By translating the bible into English and questioning the hierarchical authority of the Church he set in motion what would, a hundred years later, become the great revolution of the Reformation

Harvests were poor through much of the 14th Century. The poor and landless became increasingly restive having lost much and gained little from the plague. *'When Adam*

Bring out your dead

THE BUBONIC PLAGUE

Melcombe Regis (or Weymouth) was where the Black Death landed in England in 1349. It came from the Black Sea, borne by fleas living on rats. Each flea bite became a centre of decay with blood-filled pustules known as buboes - hence the name Bubonic Plague. Swellings under the arms and in the groin, high fever and the certainty of death within five days for three in four who caught it. It killed one third of the population.

They are like a shower of peas, the early ornaments of the black death, cinders of the peelings of the cockle weed, a mixed multitude, a black plague like halfpence, like berries.

Woe is me of the shilling in the arm pit; it is seething, terrible, wherever it may come, a head that gives pain and causes a loud cry, a burden carried under the arms, a painful angry nob, a white lump.

We see death coming into our midst like black smoke, a plague which cuts off the young, a rootless phantom which has no mercy for fair countenance.

delved and Eve span, Who was then a gentleman' was a popular ballad of the day. Wat Tyler's rebellion in 1381 brought matters to a head. There were riots in Winchester and Salisbury and doubtless Downton was affected. It was a near thing but in the end the property-owning middle and upper classes regained control.

Wyclif's followers, the Lollards, were counterattacked by the clergy and the landowners. He died in 1384, baffled though not silenced, deserted by most of his followers. His ideas however went, of all places, to Prague and from there to Martin Luther in Germany. The resulting upheaval we call the Reformation was to return to transform England - and the Church of St Laurence in Downton.

POST-TRAUMATIC STRESS

Wyclif's ideas were being absorbed by a society already under strain after the devastation of the Black Death. A third of the work force was dead. Much land was lost to cultivation. There were so few workers that they began to demand more money but this was stamped on with a wage freeze. To move away was forbidden. Although many young men defied the ban it was harder for smallholders and men with families.

Martin Luther

We believe that many of the poorer clergy were active in their villages during the epidemic because so many of them died there. It is probable that Downton's Rector was not resident as just before the Black Death he was also Master of the Hospital of St Nicholas in Winchester. It was not unusual for men to hold several Rectorships, appointing their own Vicars and Curates to carry out the pastoral work.

For the next one hundred years the Lollards continued to protest against Romish doctrine and doubtless they were heard in Downton because Salisbury was frequently the focus of their criticism and attacks. They questioned the authority of the Pope and Bishops, they wanted the Bible in

English and they were against indulgences, pilgrimages and veneration of saints and images.

In 1449 the Bishop of Chichester was killed at Portsmouth because he failed to bring the back pay for Henry VI's troops. The Bishop of Salisbury, a close adviser of the King, was murdered in 1450 near Salisbury by men from that town who went on to plunder a priory.

RICHARD II'S VISIT

In 1393 Richard II journeyed to and from Downton to Salisbury in order to have a huge party with or for the Greyfriars in Salisbury. He was an erratic and despotic King rather given to excesses and the bill for the party may explain why he stayed overnight!

BOROUGH BY PRESCRIPTION

Downton, as we have seen earlier, had long been an important centre of local government. It was a Borough by prescription rather than by Charter and that meant that its independent status had been accepted, probably from Saxon times.

From 1395 onwards, although not without interruptions, until the Reform Act of 1832, the village elected two Burgesses or Members of Parliament. To begin with they were Downton men elected by Downton men. Free Burgage tenure on the Borough and of a few houses on the island where the mills stand carried the right to vote.

MANOR OF DOWNTON

Although Downton itself survived the Black Death, it was not unaffected. The changes to more intense farming that followed to cope both with the sudden fall in the labour force and the loss of fertility of the arable fields required far more central control from the manor. New Court became the Manor House or Court Baron for those lands, including the Borough, still under the direct control of the Bishop rather than the College. It became the administrative centre in succession to Old Court.

A LOOK AROUND DOWNTON

This guide is arranged as a continuous walk and, at least at the beginning, in chronologial order. There is car parking either end and in the middle and, of course, it doesn't all have to be done at once.

❶ Site of **Mesolithic** huts and flint workings from 5,250 BC. (Not visible but it is worth looking across the river from the hardstanding in Avon Meadow - not much changed in 7,000 years)

❷ Site of **Iron Age** settlement, 1,500 BC (in playing field, not visible)

❸ Site of **Roman Villa**, 350 AD(not visible)

❹ The **Moot**. Norman motte and bailey castle built 1140 AD during the civil war between Stephen and Matilda. Two brief battles. Knocked down in Henry II's reign. Much modified in 18 and 19C. Sybil Thorndike acted on the open air stage in 1908 when thousands would visit
(Could have been fortified by Celts, Romans and Saxons but no evidence.).

❺ **Bishop's Palace** site, circa 1190. Now on the island but the millrace dates from later so it would have been part of Moot, inside the defences.(May earlier have been a Saxon Royal Villa, 7 - 11C; nothing visible.)

❻ **Moot House**. Built about 1640, rebuilt after fire in 1923. Visited by Charles I.

❼ An important crossroads. Left is the **High Street** and the oldest part of Downton. Opposite is **Barford Lane** which was the *common King's Highway* at least by 1300 and was the main road to Salisbury. The house with the timbers and rounded corner, sometimes known as the Rent House, was the last one owned by Winchester College who were given much of Downton in 1380 by the Bishop of Winchester.

❽ **Lode Hill** to the right became the main easterly road. Vine Cottage was a chantry priest's house in the 13C; the present house is later. Next to it is the old Reheboth Baptist chapel, now a garage. Up the hill, in the traffic-light controlled throat, on the right where Slab Lane comes out, you can still make out Reffel's butcher's shop signs. This house has had many uses. It may first have been the Cottage Hospital, at one stage it was used as a chapel, then by Reffells and now is private housing.

❾ Make your way in to **Barford Lane**. On the left is the old National School (i.e. a Church of England foundation), now the Church Hall. On the right is Hamilton House and beyond it is Doctor's Alley, so called because the Doctor's surgery was there for perhaps 50 years. The Alley takes the line of the original road up from the ford, past the Church and on, eventually, to London.

❿ Running beside the Church Hall and Library carpark is Snailcreep (name origin unknown) which leads to **St Laurence Church**. As you go down the path you may get glimpses through the bushes of Chalkhill House which is the old Vicarage.

St Laurence was consecrated by St Birinus, the first Bishop to the West Saxons, in 638AD. It has been rebuilt and reshaped many times since so that the oldest section we can now see dates from 1130 in Norman times. The main building seems to have been finished by 1350 although the western aisle and entrance were rebuilt in 1648.

Behind the wall on the north side of the graveyard is **Parsonage Manor**. For 100 years a branch of Sir Walter Raleigh's family lived there. Before that it may have been the Minster for the whole huge Downton parish and was certainly the first Rectory in the 14th Century.

⓫ Out through the lych gate, down the hill past an old malt house and the **King's Arms** to The Square. This is the heart of the old village with mills and inn and church and the old manor (Bishop's Palace, No 5) all close together.

⓬ Bearing right, follow the road past the **old Tannery** (now closed and being prepared for development) on the right and, **⓭** the three **mills** on the left.

⑭ You will see the **Mill Pool** on your right and then cross the **River Avon at Iron (or Catherine) Bridge.**

⑮ Having crossed the bridge, turn right along the river bank until you come out into the old **water-meadows**. No longer functioning at Downton, you can still pick out the ridges along which water was carried to sluice over the land and drain away to the river in the ditches.

⑯ Come back to the bridge and turn right in to the **Borough** noting Creel Cottage with its painted 16 and also the small carved stone inset also showing 16. Numbering of houses on the Borough mattered because Downton was entitled to two Members of Parliament from the 13th Century till 1832 and only those with burgage tenure had a vote. No.16 was making sure of its vote! It was the home of the Eastmans whose family founded Eastman Kodak.

As you come out on to the wider Green, look left at the old Workhouse.

The Borough was a 'new town' started by the Bishop of Winchester in 1209.

The model village in the front garden of a house was built to stimulate a handicapped child.

⑰ Having crossed Moulds Bridge and the New Court Carrier flowing under it, look left at **Leicester House**. 50 years ago a small bag of coins was found in a wattle and daub [mud and sticks] wall. They dated from 1309 and earlier. A Leicester was Burgess or MP for Downton at about the time the coins were hidden.

The **Borough Cross** was probably knocked down by Cromwell's New Model Army. Later reconstructions were also destroyed and in the Second World War a land mine knocked it down again. When they came to reconstruct it to mark the Coronation of Queen Elizabeth II someone found the present cross hidden nearby and masons say that it is very old. Perhaps we have the original cross back in place.

⑱ Turn left down **South Lane** past the **White Horse**. There has been a hostel or inn there since 1509, at least. As you go down South Lane you will see the **Baptist Chapel**. The Baptists in Downton go back to the 1650s. Next to the chapel is the **Court House**. On its wall you may be able to pick out a projecting carved stone on which is written Burrough and Manor with a line between. This was both the Courthouse for most of Downton and its first school and it was built in 1679 astride the boundary between Manor and Borough. Two for the price of one.

⑲ Retracing your steps and crossing the Borough, with care, look down **Gravel Close**. This was the original main road and its line runs past New Court (14C) to Charlton and so to Salisbury.

⑳ On your left is the Church of England **Primary School**. This was the Board School, built in 1895, and then the Secondary School until the new Secondary Modern School was opened in the 50's.

㉑ Continue westward down the Borough. The pillared portico of **Downton Memorial Hall** dates from after the First World War but the building behind it was built in 1840 as the British School on land leased by Lord Radnor who still owns the Greens that run down the centre of the Borough.

㉒ **The Bull** at the end of the Borough on the Headlands dates from the 18C when the present main road was opened up. Headlands derives from Hedge-land - the boundary of the common land separating pasture and crops.

㉓ Having crossed the main road at the lights, turn right. **Wick Lane** on your left is the old drovers' road, part of which is called Ox Drove, and was one of the main routes through from London to Weymouth in Saxon, Norman and mediaeval times. Down the lane is the modern Leisure Centre complex with indoor and outdoor tennis courts, badminton, bowls, football and keep-fit facilities.

㉔ Returning to the main road one can see **Long Close** opposite and this follows the line of the old road behind the Borough to where there was a hard ford to cross the river above the bridge - the reason that man settled first in Downton 7,000 years ago. New housing since the 50's gave homes to squatters who had occupied the former American Army camp where the Industrial Estate can now be seen on the left. There is a way through on foot to Gravel Close and so back to the Borough.

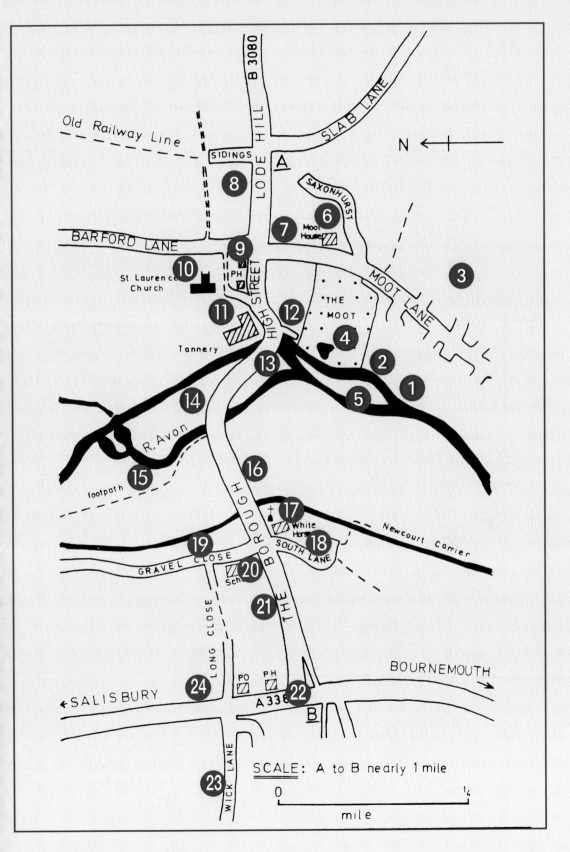

Old Railway Line

B 3080

SLAB LANE

LODE HILL

N

SIDINGS

⑧

A

SAXONHURST

⑥

⑦

Moot House

BARFORD LANE

⑨

⑩

St Laurence Church

PH

⑫

MOOT LANE

③

"THE MOOT"

⑪

HIGH STREET

④

Tannery

⑬

②

①

⑤

⑭

R. Avon

⑮

footpath

⑯

BOROUGH

⑰

White Horse

Newcourt Carrier

⑲

⑱

GRAVEL CLOSE

SOUTH LANE

⑳

Sch

THE

LONG CLOSE

㉑

BOURNEMOUTH

㉔

PO

PH

SALISBURY

㉒

A 338

B

WICK LANE

㉓

SCALE: A to B nearly 1 mile

0   ¼

mile

57

In 1551 the Bishop let the Lordship of Downton manor to a succession of Lords Lessee (or Lord Farmers). Initially to Sir William Herbert who was created Earl of Pembroke in the same year. It seems likely that the Herberts replaced the original Manor House with the eastern block of the present complex, presumably for their Steward.

New Court
seen across the valley
of the Avon and the
old water meadows

For over 100 years it stayed with the Earls until 1662 when Philip, Earl of Pembroke, was replaced by Sir Joseph Ashe as Lord Farmer. The present western block of New Court dates from the time of Sir Joseph and the Ashes and Wyndhams may have refurbished the eastern house as well. It stayed with the Ashe family until 1741.

Downton remained important to the Bishop of Winchester financially although he seems to have been a less frequent visitor. Old Court, his Palace, stayed habitable probably only until the end of the 15th Century, if then.

INFLUENTIAL ASHES - 1

Sir Joseph left his estate to his son James and it in turn passed to another Joseph Ashe more often called Ashe Wyndham or Wyndham Ashe. In 1741 it was sold to Anthony Duncombe of Barford House. On and off, Ashes were Members of Parliament for Downton from 1648 to 1742. In 1715 it could be said of Joseph Ashe that he had 50 Members of Parliament who were his relatives but he does not seem to have been representing Downton at that time

FARMING AND INDUSTRY CHANGE

We have little published information on life in Downton itself in the 300 years from the Black Death to the 17th Century. We can only conjecture that what was happening in the rest of the country applied to our village, too. Huge flocks of sheep would go up each day on to the chalk downs to feed and then, like walking dung carts, were brought down for the night to manure the cornfields.

1,000 sheep would be folded overnight on a fresh acre each day, the hurdles being moved while the sheep were away. It was the duty of the tenants to make hurdles that were also used for catching fish in the river.

In a place like Downton, farming in this way, the social organisation had to remain very strong with tenants being required to conform to the communal pasturage and folding of the bishop's sheep if they were to benefit from it. The fact that this regime was taking all the goodness out of the uplands was not understood until much later. Even the sowing and harvesting of the common lands had to be managed. Some land was let for grazing: a meadow called la Nywemede in Witherington, a small hamlet then, cost 10 shillings for a summer's grazing.

When William Fucher was outlawed for causing the death of Maude Pytte in 1249 his worldly wealth was set down. It tells us a little how one fairly ordinary peasant lived. He had a weak draught beast, two old cart wheels and one young bullock. (Was he an independent carter fallen on hard times?) He had one and a half acres sown with oats and flax and beans. This wealth was valued at sixteen shillings and five and one half pennies. [240 pennies to the pound, 12 to a shilling]

If one compares this with the 10/- rent for grazing, the dairymaid's 2/6d wages for a year or the daily wage of two and a half pennies for a skilled man like a carpenter it may not seem so bad. It is impossible to give exact equivalents because so much benefit was in kind but Fucher's capital worth seems to have been about 5 year's income. For the next 300 years it is doubtful if much changed for the ordinary peasant like him. It is a curiosity that the name of the last Hayward and Bailiff in Downton, 650 years later, was Futcher.

VARIED PRODUCE

On the demesne land, worked directly by the bishop's men, cattle, pigs, hens and rabbits were reared. The dairy probably made cheese from sheep's milk as well as cows'. It was well equipped and flourishing to judge by the quantity of salt consumed although the dairymaid was only paid two shillings and sixpence for a year's work.

Fish were required for Friday's meals so as well as letting out fishing rights the bishop would have had his own fisherman.

For Wiltshire as a whole this was a time of great expansion of the broadcloth weaving industry away from the towns. Downton's fulling mill, still owned by the Bishop, would have bought the raw wool and sent it out to cottagers to spin; the mill would then send on the yarn to the local weavers and it would be returned to be dyed and finished in the mill. From there it might either go to Salisbury to be marketed or perhaps direct to Southampton for export.

THE WATER MEADOWS ARE BUILT

As the pressure for ever higher corn production required ever more sheep, the limit became winter fodder. Eventually, to overcome this problem, water-meadows were established along the whole Avon Valley. This technical revolution did not begin until about 1635, probably on one of the Avon tributaries owned by the Earls of Pembroke.

Sir Joseph Ashe had become Lord of the Manor just as this innovation caught on and immediately set about converting the meadows north of Downton. In his case, he wanted the improved grazing for his dairy herd. Water-

Operation of the Water Meadows

Water is taken off the main river in to mini-canals - carriers. Hatches are opened to spill the water into sluices. The sluices run along the top of ridges and the water spills over the sides wetting the pasture and so keeping it from freezing. Drains in the valleys between the sluices carry the water back to the river. Warmer soil brought on the growth of grass perhaps a month early.

The right side shows the Barford system of water-meadows as it may have been; the left side is taken from a 1712 map showing the carriers, drains hatches and bargemen's bridges

Key:

≡ Stone Hatches
井 Timber Hatches
= Stop Hatches
⋊ Navigation Bridges for bargemen and horses

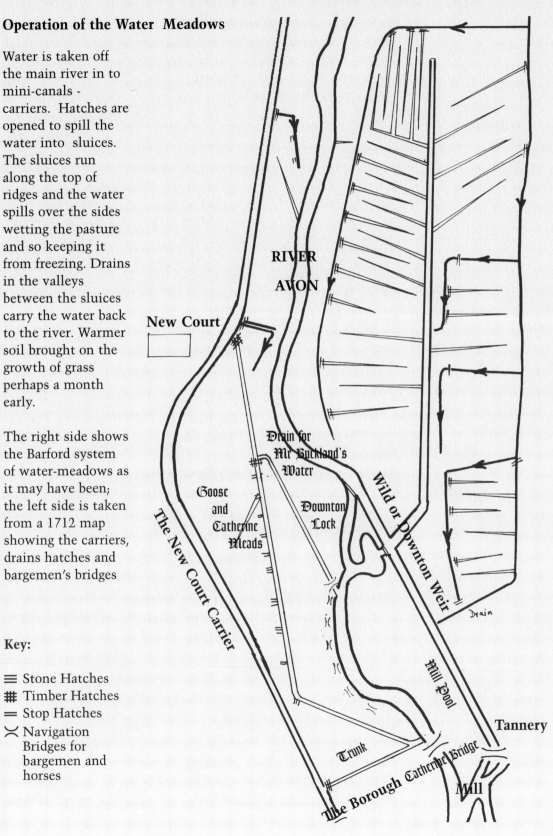

New Court

RIVER AVON

Drain for Mr Buckland's Water

Goose and Catherine Meads

Downton Lock

Wild or Downton Weir

The New Court Carrier

Drain

Mill Pool

Trunk

Tannery

The Borough   Catherine Bridge

Mill

meadows only reached south of Downton in the 1680s.

New Court controlled the construction of spillways, carriers, sluices and drains that flooded the warmer river water over the meadows, bringing it 'on at a trot and off at a gallop,' at critical times in the winter both to prevent the land freezing and to bring on an 'early bite' of lush grass perhaps a month earlier than normal in the spring. Although drowning water meadows has stopped at Downton it continues to this day at Britford a short way upstream.

There were also attempts in the later stages of this management of the river to make the Avon navigable through Downton to Salisbury but it was not ever a success. A map of the water-meadows in 1712 shows navigation bridges over the drains in to the river for the bargemen and their horses and a lock at the weir to pass the traffic up or down stream. The bridges were made of timber and close to the river where the towpath would already have been.

Chapter 4

Tudors and Others

THE REFORMATION REACHES ENGLAND......

It is important at this stage to catch up on the developments in faith and belief that paralleled the economic recovery from the Black Death.

We have looked at the continuing religious unrest starting with Wyclif and the Lollards and dissatisfaction with a rich priesthood and wealthy dominant monastic houses. It had all seemed to no avail. Henry VIII, who had been intended for the priesthood until his elder brother Arthur died, was an ardent Catholic who had earned the title Defender of the Faith, given by the Pope.

So it might have continued if Henry VIII's wife, Catherine of Aragon, had borne him a son who had survived and perhaps even then if he had found her rather more agreeable! He wanted a divorce but the Pope in Rome refused. That was not only frustrating to a strong willed man but also a direct affront to his secular, political authority in his own country. A challenge up with which he would not put, to misquote Winston Churchill, another Englishman who did not like his will crossed.

Everything began to change from 3 November 1529 when the Reformation Parliament started its sessions. Having stated the all-important principle that the King, and not the Pope, was now the head of the Church in England, the measures that followed such as the Dissolution of the Monasteries did not greatly affect ordinary people who in any case were happy to see the cleansing of a corrupt clerical regime.

.....AND EVEN DOWNTON

Churchwardens could see the way things were going and sold most of the valuable silver. This probably explains why Downton has no church plate older than 1620 - our best chalice is in the Treasury in Salisbury Cathedral, too valuable to be kept unused in the village but there as a reminder of our heritage.

In 1538 the Royal Injunctions ordered that an English bible should be set up in each church and that registers of baptisms, burials and marriages should be kept. This was immediately obeyed. One church bought 'a *boke for wrytt yn al christenynge, weddyng and beryng*' at a cost of 8 pence. In Downton's oldest surviving Register the opening page is inscribed as follows: '*This boke of Baptysme of Matrymony and of Obitts was bought* [on] *the ninth of Aprill 1599 Richard Goldston & Ambrose Snelgar beinge Churtch wardens for yt yeare*'

Cranmer

The Injunctions also ordered the removal of objects, images or paintings that could be regarded as idolatrous. Probably little actually changed at St Laurence until the reign of Edward VI. From 1547, when the nine years old King was crowned, there began a Protestant purge, under Archbishop Cranmer, which probably led in St Laurence's to the covering of the wall paintings and the removal of statuary, the stone altar and the great Rood screen at the top of the nave.

In 1549 Cranmer introduced his marvellous prayer book and, in 1551, the famous 42 Articles (later reduced to 39) which defined Anglican doctrine. We could see these today as political statements defying Rome and Spain and the rest of the Catholic world. They were to colour English thought for the next 400 years. Even today they are embedded in our language and culture however much the modernists may wish otherwise.

On succeeding Edward in 1553, Queen Mary restored Catholic worship and the Churchwardens would have had to replace their new wooden altar with a stone one and buy new plate. The Bishop of Winchester, Stephen Gardiner, had been imprisoned in the Tower by Edward who took back the Downton estate, temporarily.

Gardiner was reinstated by Mary and it was he who conducted the marriage service of the Queen with Phillip II of Spain in Winchester Cathedral. This alliance with a foreign power and the persecution of Protestants and the martyrdom of Cranmer, Latymer and Ridley were deeply resented. They were to have a profound and lasting effect on Englishmen.

When Cranmer was burnt at the stake he put his right hand in to the flames first as he was ashamed of having used it to sign papers giving the Queen support. To this day any member of the Royal Family who marries a Roman Catholic renounces his right of succession to the throne.

QUEEN ELIZABETH, THE COLLEGE AND DOWNTON

Queen Mary I

So, when Queen Elizabeth began her reign in 1558 she found a groundswell of national opinion that fitted well with her own inclinations. There was a further reversal of church usage as Mary's Roman Catholic restorations were removed. Within two years Elizabeth had had the Act of Supremacy passed. This required all clergy to acknowledge her as Supreme Governor of the Church in England. In Wiltshire only fifteen priests refused and a year later there was only one 'Popish' altar found in the whole county. Bishop Gardiner in Winchester was long gone.

As well as coping with all these upheavals the Churchwardens were given more and more, largely secular, duties. They supervised the Rogationtide beating of the bounds of the parish and were supposed to ensure regular church attendance as well as looking after vagrants and the poor.

It was a puzzling, anxious time for ordinary worshippers but their essential faith in God's power in every detail of their daily lives remained intact. A hard-headed exporter could put against each entry in his ledger *'God send it saff.'*

CLERGY AND THE CHANGES

Many of the local clergy were able to accept the switches without too much difficulty, perhaps rightly seeing the cure of souls as their first charge. They varied from semi-educated men little different to the farmers they served to wealthy patricians, the younger sons of nobility. Some readers will know the song *The Vicar of Bray* which recites in many verses how he trimmed and bent with the wind through all the changes and so remained the Vicar of Bray.

We know that the Vicars of Downton were often educated men, Doctors of Divinity or Masters of Arts. In the latter half of Elizabeth's reign, in 1585, Rev. William *Wilkes* DD became Vicar and, if the records are right, he stayed in office for fifty years, a steadying influence after a time of great stress for all.

THE RALEIGHS GET PARSONAGE MANOR

Sir Walter Raleigh

In 1581 the lease of Parsonage Manor had been reluctantly ceded by the Governors of Winchester College to Queen Elizabeth for 40 years. The Queen gave the lease of the Parsonage to Thomas *Wilkes*, her Clerk of the Privy Council, who held it till he died in 1598.

There is here a coincidence of names and dates that catches the eye. Whether Sir *Thomas* Wilkes, a power in the land, came to some deal with the College over the appointment of Rev. *William* Wilkes, his cousin, we do not know but Thomas was a man to keep in with. William Wilkes was to become preacher both to Queen Elizabeth and to James I.

Although the Queen may have visited Downton it is likely that the Vicar usually relied on a curate to serve his

Downton flock while he lived elsewhere.

The Parsonage was sub-let to various people and it was not until 1626 that the College passed the lease directly to the Raleigh family.

It seems that the Raleighs may actually have been living there almost from the beginning of the Crown's lease and presumably paid rent to whichever landlord currently held the sub-lease. From 1647 to 1686 Gilbert Raleigh was the leaseholder. The Raleighs remained there over 100 years. It looks as though they only left after the death of Sir Charles Raleigh in 1698. Raleighs were MPs for Downton periodically until 1701.

RICH BREWERS

The Raleighs were nothing if not enterprising. While Sir Walter plagued the Spaniards, his brother's family went into brewing and perhaps wine making and trading. In the cellar at Parsonage Manor there are the remains of the brewery or *brewehouse*. In Sir Charles Raleigh's 1698 Inventory after his death there were at least 70 *'hoggesheads'* of various beers and ales - that is over 30,000 pints - and at least 2,200 bottles of wine, presumably much of it, if not all, imported.

The contents of the 35 rooms and spaces listed is evidence of startling wealth. 26 leather seated chairs in the Hall although none in the *Great Parler*. At the end we catch a glimpse of the underlying wealth of this man because he had £2,000 in Bank of England Stock and £1,000 in 14% Exchequer Annuities and his total assets were £4,687. That would make him a multi-millionaire in our time.

Parsonage Manor

The Queen receives foreign Ambassadors

Earl of Leicester is one of the courtiers

WINCHESTER, DOWNTON AND THE QUEEN

On one side of the stage **Queen Elizabeth** is enthroned. Close to her are the **Earl of Leicester** and other courtiers and attendants. **Leicester** occasionally crosses to a table to write. Opposite, sometimes facing her, sometimes conferring among themselves, are the **Warden** and **Fellows** of Winchester College.

Somehow the Queen has heard that the College has recently gained possession of Parsonage Manor in Downton and decides that this holding would suit her as a present to Thomas Wilkes, Clerk of her Privy Council, one of a small group round her who did the administrative work of her government. She has written to the Warden saying this is what she wants and offering a very low rent for 40 years but has had no reply. **Leicester** has penned a follow up letter recommending compliance - or else!

LEICESTER, reading the letter to the Queen: **"With my hearty commendations. You shall understand that the Queen's Majesty at her special favour and right good deserving of Mr Wilkes, Clerk of Her Majesty's Council, hath whryte to you and your company for lease....**

The Fellows are listening intently to the Warden who continues reading the letter.

WARDEN: 'for a lease in reversion to be made over to herself and so to be made in like sort to the said gentleman her servant at her pleasure...'

1st FELLOW: 'What! "At her pleasure" indeed!'

2nd FELLOW: 'Hush. Read on Warden.'

WARDEN, adjusting position to get more light: "As it is not unlike that you and the rest will be well content to gratifye Her Majestye in so reasonable request...'

1st FELLOW: 'Reasonable request!'

WARDEN: 'So hence I thought good to let you understand the good opinion that Her Majestye had conceived of the seyde Mr Wilkes her servant and also of the place he serves in ...'

2nd FELLOW: 'No doubt he does think good to let us know'.

WARDEN: "which I doubt not that it is sufficient to

persuade you to fulfil her request" Oh dear, this light is no longer favourable to my eyes (beckoning to one of the younger Fellows) Partridge, dear boy, your eyes are youthful - come and read the rest of this missive so that the Fellows may know Her Majesty's Pleasure.'

PARTRIDGE: "which otherwise, if not Her Majesty had written, both myself and others of Her Majesty's Councillors had of themselves favour of the gentleman knowing his worthyness and well deserving...."

WARDEN, tetchily: 'Yes, yes, certainly he is most worthy and deserving, Partridge, but is there any more meat in this letter, you can spare us the dressing.'

PARTRIDGE, hastily scanning the rest of the letter: 'ummm..."Whereby it will appear unto you upon your conformity Her Majesty's thankful acceptance thereof and thus will I cease for this time and recommend you to the Grace of God..."

1st FELLOW, furious: 'As well he might.'

PARTRIDGE: "...at Court this 17th day of January fifteen hundred and eighty one."

Silence. The Fellows look at one another in dismay.

WARDEN: 'Barnaby, remind me how large is our manor at Downton?'

BARNABY: 'It is 194 acres of good land by the river, Warden.'

WARDEN: 'And the house?'

BARNABY: 'The house stands by the church and is of a goodly size. Shuffling through some papers.

It was leased to the Earl of Pembroke and then until a couple of months ago, to John Stockman, Esquire. So, at the moment, it is vacant.'

WARDEN: 'How does she know these things - oh! I expect it is those Herberts at Wilton. No matter. Is there any way out of this loss. He looks around the silent, troubled fellows. **I have spent much of the night pondering this and can find no answer save compliance. We'll meet again this day sennight. Perhaps the Lord will show us a way out of this dangerous maze.'**

Back to the Court. **Leicester** and the **Queen** are flirting but evidently business goes on.....

LEICESTER: 'But Ma'am!'

QUEEN: 'I will have no 'buts', Robert. Wilkes is waiting. Where is the Downton Manor?'

LEICESTER: 'The Fellows have advised me that it has pleased God to call their venerable Warden away to His bosom.....

QUEEN: 'How very convenient for them!'

LEICESTER: '....and being aware of their duty to your gracious self....'

QUEEN: 'Of course.'

LEICESTER: '...they are at this moment electing their new Warden.'

QUEEN: 'And who will that be?'

LEICESTER: 'It is a secret election'

QUEEN: 'My Lord of Leicester, I fear that you are losing your faculties! You doubtless did not hear me aright. I asked who was to be the new Warden of Winchester College.'

LEICESTER: 'Dr Bilson, I believe, Your Majesty.'

QUEEN: 'Indeed....will we have any trouble with Dr Bilson?'

LEICESTER: 'I think not, Ma'am.'

The Queen laughs and they talk sotto voce as the scene shifts to the Fellows. **Dr Bilson** is sitting in the Warden's chair reading from the next letter from Court.

BILSON: "And to that end you are hereby required, upon receipt hereof, that you do accordingly seal and confirm to Her Majesty the said lease … which we doubt not that you will dutifully perform according to your promise contained in your former letters."

1st FELLOW: 'Our promise, indeed. Pure coercion.'

2nd FELLOW: 'There is nothing for it but to assent?'

BILSON: 'I fear not.'

1st FELLOW: 'If the Queen's Majesty sees fit to denude the College of its property at such favourable terms to herself how are we to support our scholars?'

BILSON: 'Gentlemen, I have given much thought to this matter. As I see it, there is nothing that can be done about the manor at Downton without the appearance of treason. However, if we bend before the might of Her Gracious Majesty's August presence then… in the future…we just may be able to preserve some other of our lands.'

3rd FELLOW: 'How, pray, do you propose to accomplish such a feat of diplomacy?'

BILSON: 'With honey, my dear Hatton, with a great deal of honey!'

Back to the **Queen** and **Leicester**. **Leicester** is reading the Warden's letter to the Queen.

QUEEN: 'Continue, Robert.'

LEICESTER: 'We, the Warden and Fellows and Scholars, clerks of this College, have confirmed the lease unto Your Highness…'

QUEEN: 'Aah.....for how long?'

LEICESTER: 'For forty years… of the patronage and Rectory of Downton in the county of Wiltshire…'

QUEEN: 'Excellent....most satisfactory...'

LEICESTER: 'There is more, Your Majesty'

QUEEN immediately on guard: 'More? What more else could they possibly want to say?'

LEICESTER: 'They want you to agree not to ask them to provide property at cut prices, Ma'am, if I may put it that way...'

QUEEN: 'Do they indeed? So how do they word such a rash idea, pray?

LEICESTER: 'Very prettily, Your Highness.'

QUEEN, laughing: 'Let me see how these learned gentlemen turn their hand to courtly compliments (takes the letter from Leicester's hand) "We do most humbly desire and beseech your Most Excellent Majesty"...good..."by your Majesty's princely affection towards the maintenance of learning".... very good.... aha..."Be a sufficient occasion to make a stay of like suits to be tendered by any person".....there we have it....the very pith and substance of their argument....and again.. "a particular mark of Your Majesty's most gracious good meaning to discharge us of the hazard of decay of our maintenance"...dear, dear... Do you think they are going to starve, Robert?'

LEICESTER: 'I doubt that, Ma'am'

QUEEN, laughing and reading on: 'Oh, but I must agree to this request...harken to this "and as a true Mother of all virtue and true learning, to yield unto us a defence against all other attempts..."

Who else would take their lands if not myself? And they appeal to my Own Gracious Majesty to protect themselves from My Acquisitive Majesty! I salute you, Dr Bilson! A worthy adversary.'

Laughs and throws the letter at Leicester 'We will leave these scholars to their books and their lands ..... it's time for less weighty matters.' They exit with him holding her hand in a courtier's deferential but intimate grasp, both laughing and in high spirits.

CHALKHILL HOUSE

William Wilkes' successor in 1637, fifty years later, was John Chalkhill and in 1640 he built or rebuilt the Vicarage which had moved from Parsonage Manor, also next to the Church. Today it is called Chalkhill House but what one sees facing the lawn was built by a later Vicar, Thomas Lear, who took out a mortgage for £450 to do the work in 1784. A house had been there since 1385 when an acre was set aside from the Rector's land for it. In a dry summer the outline of foundations for a three-roomed building can be seen on the lawn. Possibly the old Vicarage was not up to the standard Chalkhill required. The living had lost much of its revenue but it certainly looks as though men of quality and means still sought it.

DOWNTON TRADESMEN

Odd glimpses of life in Downton come from licensing records and magistrates' court proceedings of the late 16th and early 17th Centuries. Central government had progressively interfered more and more in the economic life of the country partly as regulators and partly to raise revenue.

Many of the surviving reports are of misdeeds, alleged or real. In 1577 John Lecyter the Elder was fined one sixth of a pound(3/4d) by John Eyer and Aemy Clifford, JPs, for 'batterey of Ellen Justian.' This is of added interest because, as mentioned earlier, we have Leicester House still in the centre of the Borough, a William Leicester was representing Downton in Parliament in 1301, and because the probable descendants of John Eyer are living at Newhouse today.

John Eastman [probably from Downton but there were other Eastmans at Charlton and Nunton] was indicted by Robert Bedoe of London, yeoman, for buying sheep for 20 shillings and lambs at 10 shillings each and selling them in Westminster within five weeks. Presumably at great profit and without adding any value by first fattening them *and illegal*. He protested his innocence but was fined just the same.

In 1612 William Stockman, Edward Fauston and Henry Welstead of Downton were turned in for engrossing (cornering) wheat, barley and oats. Stockman was probably the holder of Barford from Winchester College as well as parts of the Bishop of Winchester's Downton estate and the man who founded Stockman's Charity in 1626. That charity, now combined with others, survives to this day and makes small grants to the needy and elderly.

INFORMERS AND ENGROSSERS

It was a lucrative trade to inform on lawbreakers. Informing was often run as a business by London entrepreneurs as they could collect half the money or goods fined. They operated as a very corrupt commercial police force thriving on the multiplicity of laws that could be broken.

'Engrossing' was a particular favourite of theirs because the pickings were so good. An engrosser was a middleman who cornered the market, buying up the bulk of a product in an area so as to put up the price. If convicted under an Act of 1552 he went to prison for 2 months and lost all his goods; for a second offence, 6 months and twice the value of the goods and for a third offence, life imprisonment, the pillory and his entire estate forfeited.

KING'S CLERK OF THE MARKET

Weights and measures, quality of merchandise, rules for apprenticeship - no one could be a baker unless he had seven years training - all were subject to the King's Clerk of

Too much engrossing ...

the Market. This office was maintained for 500 years, starting simply as the official who paid suppliers of food directly to the Court rather than through middlemen in order to save the King money.

We can imagine the drovers taking their cattle up the road from Downton to Clarendon Palace or to Wilton and being paid by this official. We know that after King John had stayed at Clarendon in 1209 he made payments to the Bishop of Winchester, Peter de Roches.

DOWNTON DRINKING HOLES

There were a bewildering variety of places where you could get a drink and each had to be licensed. Old English ale had been supplanted by beer brewed with hops in the 1520s and this was a much headier quaff. **Inns** were primarily for travellers although they also sold wine and beer to locals. **Taverns** were wine shops but sold food and drink for consumption on the premises. **Alehouses** sold only ale and beer. Finally, a **tippling-house** was a low class alehouse.

Widows were encouraged to open taverns and alehouses in their homes so that they did not become a burden on the parish. Perhaps the equivalent today would be running Bed and Breakfast. A *'keeper of an ordinary table'* ran a restaurant.

WHITE HORSE IN GOOD FOOD GUIDE OF 1617?

Although English inns were much criticised at home, Fynes Morison, who had travelled widely in Europe, could make this comment in 1617: *'The world affordes not such Innes as England hath for good and cheap entertainment, after the Guests own pleasure, or for humble attendance upon passengers; yea even in very poor villages.'* So, "Well done" to the 'White Horse' of 1617 - for it was well established by then, by that name. There are many reasons to think it was in fact also the unnamed hostel mentioned in the 13th and 15th Centuries and Anne Maple's inn seeing off the competition in 1576.

In 1576 Anne Maple was keeping the Inn in Downton and she persuaded the magistrates to make an injunction for others to *'leave of.'* *'All the rest that toke upon them to kepe eny Inne in Downton to leave of and receave no more horses nor horsemen nethr fotemen....'*

In 1590 John Jennings was fined 5 shillings (the church tithe for Downton - roughly equivalent to the rates - was 1 shilling in 1579) although he pleaded not guilty to keeping an alehouse without a licence. John Snelgar, husbandman, was fined the same amount although he too pleaded not guilty.

The Snelgars or Snelgroves had come from Fisherton Delamere to Downton in 1551. The circumstances are unclear but Margaret Snelgrove, widow of William, took the lease of part of Thrings farm which later was called Moot Farm. Her eldest son, Robert, held much of Redlynch Manor and a son-in-law held Templemans Farm. Edmund, another son, was a tanner. They feature in Downton's very first church Register.

Margaret's Will in 1560 shows her to have been a comparatively wealthy woman. She leaves money to the *'high awlter'*, *'Rep'ations of my p'h church of Downton'* and for *'the mending of Catheren Brydge in Downton.'* Having disposed of her valuable furniture, silver, bed linen and clothing to children and god-daughters, she leaves *'my kyne my oxen my cartt horses and xl[40] sheep'* to her youngest son Thomas who was probably still getting on his feet commercially. His older brothers got less.

A great-grand daughter married a Giles Eyre *'of Sarum.'*

Edmund, the tanner, had his tanyard near where the main carriage is now bridged in the Borough but this was before water meadows had been constructed and there may have been difficulty in getting enough water for their factory. It seems that his sons were out of tanning before they died. We find Peter Coles negotiating terms for his tanyard when Sir Joseph Ashe excavates the main carriage for his new watermeadows in 1665.

Coles sells on to Joseph Davies in 1717 and Davies is still there in 1745 but may be the last on the Borough - other properties between the White Horse and Moulds Bridge are described as *'formerly tanshouses.'* Davies' wife seems to have provoked him sorely as we shall see when we come to how Downton was governed and policed.

The Snelgroves remained relatively well-to-do, and in the 18th Century one of them set up a paper mill in Downton. Some still live in Downton and Redlynch.

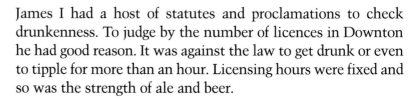

POLITICAL CORRECTNESS 400 YEARS AGO

A contemporary could say *'A wife in England is de jure* [in law] *but the best of servants, having nothing in a more proper sense than a child hath,....their condition de facto [in fact] is the best in the world, such is the good nature of Englishmen toward their wives.'* This was true although not necessarily for the reason given! Households were by this time the principal economic productive unit. Wives were No.2 in the firm, kept the accounts and stood in for their husbands when away. They often continued to run the business if their husbands died. Marriage was therefore an important step, the setting up of an independent business for those of *'the middling sort.'* A good dowry was often more important than good looks.

JAMES TIGHTENS THE SCREW

James I had a host of statutes and proclamations to check drunkenness. To judge by the number of licences in Downton he had good reason. It was against the law to get drunk or even to tipple for more than an hour. Licensing hours were fixed and so was the strength of ale and beer.

In 1619 he had forbidden the eating of meat in Lent and on Fridays throughout the year.

To begin with this was effective only in big towns but in 1620 we know of 2 Inns, I Tavern, 1 Alehouse and 2 Tipplers in Downton because they had had to swear to comply with King James' proclamations on pain of losing a large deposit, paid beforehand to the Exchequer, if they broke the rules.

Nobody knows how the two *licensed* butchers in Downton survived this complete stoppage of their trade for over a month - a good deal worse than just not being allowed to sell beef 'on the bone' today. Other tradesmen we know of at that time are bakers (often in trouble for baking spice buns - also illegal in Lent), weavers and linen weavers, tanners and shoemakers.

PARSONAGE MANOR UPLIFT

There is a story that the Raleighs were alarmed to hear that the Queen intended to take lunch with them at Downton on her way through to see the fine new house at Breamore. Parsonage Manor, or whatever it was then called, was little more than a barn - a great hall, if one wanted to be generous - and not up to standard for a Queen.

She was known to take personal hygiene very seriously; indeed, her favourite Godson, Sir John Harington, had invented the water closet for her while also finding time to translate naughty Roman plays and fight in Ireland - typical Elizabethan man. Lady Harington was typically Elizabethan in another way. Her portrait shows her wearing the skins of over 3,000 ermine that probably had been caught in Russia in midwinter. Such conspicuous consumption of wealth was accepted and expected as the Raleighs well knew.

The legend, and it may well have been embellished over the years, is that Sir Walter Raleigh had an old ship towed up the Avon and that a great refurbishment was hastily put through using its salt-sodden timbers. Whether every modern convenience was provided for the Queen we are not told although a blocked up hole in the wall is said to have been its site. Certainly, it was at this time that most of the second storey of rooms was created. One architectural historian believes that the original 14th Century roof timbers mostly survived. Whatever their age, they are a joy to behold.

Some ship's timbers _are_ there and the house _was_ brought up to a high standard. Some of the cottages in the Borough also make claims to ship's timbers. Nothing was wasted.

A full length portrait of the great explorer and pirate, Sir Walter Raleigh, was found behind panelling in the _Great Parler_ and is now in the National Portrait Gallery in London. It was the Gallery's first purchase, for £100 guineas, and only its 5th painting ever.

However, there is no mention in the extensive contemporary records at Breamore House of the Queen's stay there. The Hulse family, still living at Breamore, believe she did visit but did not stay. She often stayed at Wilton House with the Herberts so a day trip would have been easy to either Breamore or Downton.

LENTEN FASTING

King James had a particular obsession with Lenten fasting. We hear of him in 1620 going to St Paul's to hear a sermon on Mid-Lent Sunday. On his last visit to St Paul's he had noticed a tippling house and a tobacconist by the West Gate so he had instructed the Bishop of London to have them razed to the ground before his next visit - which they had been.

DOWNTON MILLERS

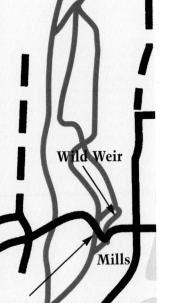

Its mills had a great influence on the life of Downton. In 1086 the Bishop of Winchester had had seven of them on his Downton estate but several of those would not have been in Downton itself.

Some of those in Downton appear always to have been where they are today, opposite the tannery and between the old village and the Borough. The leet supplying water to them was taken off the Avon some 400 meters upstream. An even greater head of water was created by the reconstruction of Wild Weir which in 1647 was said to be 200 metres long. Presumably a few years later it was further modified to accommodate the new system of water meadows. The Manor Mill had been at Wild Weir but was moved to join the others.

Perhaps when an additional mill was built about 1247 a channel was cut below the mill race between the Moot and Old Court to take the used water away quickly. The mills remained in the Bishop's gift. When Queen Elizabeth 'persuaded' the Bishop to lease the Parsonage Manor to her for forty years the mills came with it. They were in Sir Thomas Wilkes' name in 1593. There were by then two corn mills, a malting mill to grind the mash for beer or ale and, since 1215, a fulling mill to cleanse and thicken the cloth woven in the area, one of the first in Wiltshire.

FULLING

For several centuries fulling, which consisted of hammering cloth that had fullers' earth embedded in it till it felted and so became much more wind and waterproof, was the only part of cloth manufacture that was mechanised.

FLOODING

The miller and his wife

Flooding of the flat land either side of the River Avon must always have happened. Much of the Borough must have been vulnerable even when the Bishop set up his new town there but the weather in the 13th Century was particularly good so perhaps the threat seemed remote. Raising weirs to give a head of water for mills, the engineering of water meadows and, more recently, fish farms constricted flow deliberately. So much so that Downton qualifies for a major flood alleviation scheme although global warming and coastal defences seem likely to defer work on it till *after* rather than *before* the disaster it is designed to prevent.

We know there were floods in Downton in 1606 which lasted over a month with passage only possible by boat. Floods again in 1636 because the burgage tenants complained of them when pleading their poverty, no doubt to avoid or reduce some tax. The prosperous part of the village was round the mills and up the High Street at this time.

Thomas Snelgrove kept a Day Book or diary in which early entries are:

January 29th 1791 *Married this day Thos. Snelgrove to Elizabeth Bloomer Thor.*

May 18th 1791 *Downton election settled with Bovery & Scott and Shafto & Rightson. The news came on Wednesday.*

June 12th 1794 *Downton lewmeneated for the battle of Lord Howe and French fleet.* ['Glorious First of June'. James Chalk, a Downton diarist in 1869, noted the 75th anniversary with an 'I remember it well' comment.]

> January 27th 1795 *Water risen*
> January 28th 1795 *1 day flud.*
> February 9th and 10th *Second flud.*
> February 1st 1796 *Done nothing waitin for a fludd.*
> February 4th 1796 *Done nothing high water.*

The Borough floods ...

Flooding sufficient to stop Borough traffic and flood some homes occurs on average every five years. Mr Hickman whose grain store, now a block of flats, was at the end of the Borough just short of Iron Bridge, was so inured to the water that he sat in his office in his rubber boots doing his paperwork, regardless.

... so does everywhere else!

There have been at least ten bad floods in the 20th Century. In 1961 Mrs Eastman would recall 1915 especially: **'Remember how we all had privies in the garden, all awash.'** In 1990 it was back to boats with two people marooned and in 1999 the lorries that persisted in ploughing through the floods on the Borough swept water in to nearby houses that would otherwise have been flood-free.

INFLUENTIAL ASHES - 2

Although the Ashes held Downton and did a great deal in and around Downton they also lived at Twickenham and we have a note from there to Mr Snowe, the Downton Steward, which shows how people like Sir Joseph operated. Dated 20 October 1701 it goes: *"You must speak to Mrs Hayter forthwith to putt up four pots of butter, each pot to hold 20 lbs weight and send as soon as ever she can. She must see to do it up very nicely. He desires that she continue to send the fowls she spoke of beginning of next December and that she get him 4 flitches of best bacon".*

STOCKMAN'S CHARITY

Both John and William Stockman have been mentioned. The Stockmans held Barford Park and much other land both in Parsonage Manor and the Manor of East Downton. The Stockman Charity was established in 1626 by William Stockman. It was endowed with 6 cottages and 60 acres at Whiteparish (next door village to Downton, to the east) called Chadwell Grounds and Stillman Moor. The income was to be applied for the relief of certain poor persons in Downton. Specifically, it was to go to poor workers with large families and was to be paid in quarterly instalments. It was <u>not</u> to go to the Poor Box.

By 1794 some of it had been converted into £300 of 3% Government Stock. In the years up to 1832 it was able to distribute £40 a year which was the annual rent of Chadwell Farm. It is interesting to contemplate the value today of 6 cottages and 60 acres - probably not less than £250,000. It could today have been producing an annual income of around £11,000 but instead it has been swallowed up by inflation. The Charity itself survives to this day, making small annual donations.

Chapter 5

Challenge and Change

POLITICAL AND RELIGIOUS REVOLUTION

The Stuarts never truly understood their subjects and the fragile but real national unity under Queen Elizabeth gradually broke down. Under King James I and King Charles I the tensions were more openly political. Downton was, like much of England, an unwilling bystander dragged in to a nasty squabble.

King Charles I

CIVIL WAR

In 1642 Charles I stayed a night at Moot House, newly built, which belonged then to the Shuckburgh family. The King was on his way to join his army in Oxfordshire. He enlisted Sir Richard Shuckburgh who was with him at the battle of Edgehill, one of the first in the Civil War that was to end Charles' rule.

Sir Richard, making his way back to Downton, was captured by the Parliamentarians and sent to Kenilworth as a prisoner. He had to pay a large fine to get his release. There is a Shuckburgh memorial in the South transept.

England went from great prosperity to desperate poverty in those terrible 15 years of the Civil War, Commonwealth and Restoration of Charles II. The nearest battles were at Winchester and Basing.

Cromwell narrowly escaped being killed in a skirmish at Longford Castle. It is said that Royalist soldiers under Sir Thomas Hooper were camped in the Great Barn at New Court - some got married while there and others died, in one case after a fight with another soldier.

Cromwell's Seal

Few places avoided the depredations of one army or the other. So much so that many locals joined together as the Clubmen to oppose whoever wanted to take their produce.

'If you offer to plunder or take our cattle
Be assured we will give you battle'
was inscribed on one of the Clubmen's banners.

Cromwell campaigned all over England with his New Model Army

CROMWELL TAKES LONGFORD HOUSE

In October 1645 Oliver Cromwell laid siege to Longford House. He wrote to Speaker Lenthall reporting its surrender by Sir Bartholomew Pell, commander-in-chief of Longford, to Colonel Hewson and Major Kelsey. All arms were to be surrendered *'without imbezeling'*. 15 officers were to be allowed to ride out still with swords and pistols, the men were to be escorted towards Oxford (where the King's army was based) and a final 14 officers were to be allowed to leave with light arms later.

COMMONWEALTH PAINS

The troubles were not over when the war ended. The Bishop of Winchester, a committed Royalist, lost his Downton estates until Charles II came back to claim the throne. Some of the best standing timber was to be sold off but this was stopped as it might be needed by the Navy.

Adam and Eve and Noah's Ark from a pictorial Bible

The ordinary people of Downton would have had to adjust to the imposition of a Presbyterian regime in their church. Whatever remained of Catholic images and glass in the church may well have been destroyed by the Puritans at this time (there is a suggestion that even more havoc was caused by the Victorian architect T H Wyatt, whose older cousin so savaged Salisbury Cathedral, when he 'restored' St Laurence in the 19th Century.) It is thought that the Borough Cross may have been struck down by Cromwell's New Model Army - the present Cross dates from well before that time and was found half-buried nearby.

It is a curiosity that the south aisle and present porch of St Laurence Church date from 1648 in the middle of this terrible time. People in Downton would have suffered as trade collapsed and harsh taxes were imposed. It was a bitter time. Many lived on starvation or near-starvation diets, deaths increased, and births declined.

A RALEIGH IN TROUBLE

Dr Raleigh, elder brother of Sir Walter, chaplain to the Earl of Pembroke at Wilton and Dean of Wells must have sorely provoked the Roundheads and Levellers because he was captured in the Civil War and stripped of all his wealth. In 1645, as a very old man, he was taken to Bridgwater as a prisoner and given into the care of a vicious and cruel shoemaker who often beat him and finally stabbed him, causing his death.

THE EYRES AND NEWHOUSE

Thomas Eyre was one of three nominated representatives from Wiltshire in the Commonwealth Parliament of 1653, often called the Barebones Parliament after one of its members, Praisegod Barebones. 'Nominated,' not 'elected,' as Cromwell, Lord Protector, was not ready to trust the people with elections but did not want to be an absolute dictator and refused to be King.

Thomas Eyre is not listed in any of the thirteen powerful committees set up by that Parliament to regulate such diverse matters as Scotland, the advancement of Learning and receiving Petitions. It must be likely that he was from the Eyre family of Downton and Hamptworth. William Eyre of Newhouse had been an MP for Downton in Charles I's Parliament and a Gyles Eyre of Brickworth was an MP for Downton in 1660 in Charles II's reign.

Newhouse was built some time before 1619. There is dispute whether it was built by Stockman of Barford or by Sir Edward Gorges, the owner of Longford Castle, to whom Stockman had sold the land. What is not in doubt is that Gorges sold Newhouse in 1633 to Giles Eyre of Brickworth who gave it to his second son, Ambrose. Ambrose sold it to his cousin, Sir Samuel Eyre, whose descendants live there still. The house may have been a hunting lodge and is an unusual 'Y' shape. The arms of the Y were considerably extended with fine rooms decorated with high quality plaster work in the 18th and 19th Century.

Newhouse, Redlynch

GYLES EYRE: 'A VILLAGE HAMPDEN'

In Whiteparish church there is an inscription that reads in part:

'Buried here Gyles Eyre Esqre and Jane his wife. A man much oppressed by publick power for his laudable opposition to the measures taken in the reigns of James I and Charles I In the year 1640 ... he was plundered of 2000£ value and imprisoned for refusing to pay the sum of 400£ illegally demanded of him by two instruments under the Privy Seal at Oxford, 14 February 1643. He was Baptised February 1572, dyed January 1655 having issue seven sons (three of whom were likewise members of parliament) and four daughters.'

STANDLYNCH PLOTTERS

In March 1655 Colonel John Penruddock lead a Royalist rising in Salisbury in support of Charles II. It was a total failure and Penruddock was beheaded. Penruddocks had been MPs for Downton in 1570 and 1601.

Standlynch Manor had been held by the Bocklands since 1585 and it was said to be there that a number of local people gathered to organise themelves for Penruddock's action. This is plausible as Bockland was a Royalist and married to Penruddock's sister. A John Hely got wind of it and told the other side.

By 1661 the Bocklands were clearly back as two of them were MPs for Downton until 1690. They sold Standlynch in 1726 to Sir Peter Vandeput who built a fine new house on the hill above where the dilapidated old Manor stood.

PAPIST PLOTTERS

"The information of James Hely, of Sarum, in the County of Wilts saith:

'that on the 12th March last, being the day of the rising at Sarum, there were seen at Mr Brocklands' of Stanlynch in the said County, some ten horsemen in a party, with swords by their sides, among which were Sir William Courtney, Sir Charles Blount, Sir Alex Carne and one Mr Raleigh of Downton, this being according to the relation of a Justice of the Peace for the said County. Witness my hand the 17th July 1655:- Ja. Hely

These were all Papists, and the party at whose house they were seen of the same religion."

Chapter 5 Challenge and Change

The Bible in English transformed English thought. A literal interpretation became important in developing Nonconformist doctrine ...

The plagues in Egypt ... the slaughter of cattle

... the first born slain

The Red Sea parts to allow the Israelites to escape from Egypt, Pharaoh pursuing

Manna from Heaven

Chapter 6

Baptists and Landlords

CHANGE IN THE AIR

Two processes had begun even before the Reformation that now, at the end of the 17th Century, seem to have accelerated around Downton.

One was the growth of big landed estates. Wealthy landowners were replacing the Bishop and the College as the controllers of Downton. They competed for influence, buying up as many vote-carrying burgages as possible so as to be able to nominate who should be the two MPs for Downton. We shall see their influence too in St Laurence Church.

The other, only in part a reaction to the restoration of worldliness in the church, was the growth of Nonconformist worship. It is these that we now look at in Downton.

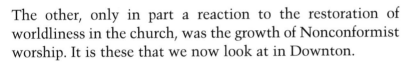

BAPTIST BEGINNINGS

The earliest English Baptist church had been founded by John Smyth in Amsterdam in 1608 whence he and others had emigrated to escape persecution. Others there were the English Separatists who had left at the end of Elizabeth's reign. At the same time several of the English Plantations or colonies in America were started for the same reason. Between 1630 and 1643 20,000 were shipped to New England and Maine while another 40,000 went to Virginia. Three quarters died early but they had free land and freedom and Rev Hugh Peters could say in 1645 *'in seven years I never saw a beggar, nor heard an oath, nor looked upon a drunkard.'*

DOWNTON BAPTISTS

One group of the Amsterdam Baptist exiles under the leadership of Thomas White is known to have come from the Downton area. It is possible that one of them, Cuthbert Hutton, a pewterer, came from Downton itself. It is thought that it was these emigrés who were instrumental in getting John Smyth's books up the Avon Valley. These and, perhaps, the return of some of the exiles, led to the

Several of the pictures in this and the previous chapter are from old editions of John Bunyan's 'Pilgrim's Progress'

NONCONFORMISTS AND THE ESTABLISHMENT

The ferment started by Wyclif 300 years earlier led on to the Reformation and the Protestant revolution that ebbed and flowed with successive monarchs, often with bloody consequences.

Although the Civil War was ultimately political - would Parliament or the King prevail - there was also an underlying religious divide in the country between Church of England Royalists and the Puritan Roundheads who ranged from low church Anglicans to the very intolerant New Model Army Presbyterians. Catholics were excluded from public life and if they refused to attend the Established Church they were called 'recusant' and at some times suffered fines or worse.

founding of General Baptist churches at Fordingbridge, Downton and Salisbury - in Salisbury this was as early as 1626.

The earliest Downton gatherings of Baptists were at night on the Downs above Wick. The first Baptist congregation in Downton is believed to have existed during the Protectorate (1653-58). In 1662 a small group of them was led by Peter Coles, the tanner. One of their number was called Mary Peenhorne which suggests that she and others may indeed have come back from Holland. That would also explain why they were General rather than Particular Baptists.

DOWNTON'S FIRST BAPTIST CHAPEL

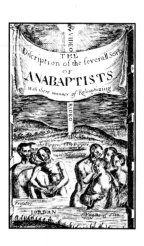

In 1680 John Sanger was the minister with Peter Coles his assistant. Both were constantly at odds with the Bishop of Salisbury and Coles was imprisoned for several years in Fisherton gaol despite Charles II's 1672 Declaration of Indulgence that allowed dissenters to obtain a royal licence to worship. For some reason Downton's church did not do this.

John Sanger was also probably the schoolmaster in Ashe and Eyre's Free School (of which more later) as he is known to have kept a grammar school and there was only one. He had a hard time. There was much persecution of nonconformists under the Conventicle Act, 1664. This was the time of the Restoration of Charles II, always a bit cagey

about his religious orientation, and of James II who was openly Catholic.

The Establishment of the day saw this new way of worshipping, which rejected the authority of the hierarchy of the Church of England, in the belief that each had a direct and personal relationship with God, in much the same way that, in our time, we saw Communism. It was a threat to their power and values.

GENERAL OR PARTICULAR

General Baptists held to a universal or *'general'* view of the atonement whereas Particular Baptists had decided that the atonement was only for those *'particularly'* chosen by God for salvation and in their view that was them! The Amsterdam exiles* had stuck closer to Smyth's original teaching but those who set up independently in England faced such persecution that a more exclusive interpretation is hardly surprising.

*nicknamed *'the Amsterdamnables'* by opponents!

It is a feature of these early Baptist congregations that they embraced all sorts, many of them with quite a lot to lose in the *'sufferings'* they experienced for not conforming with the strict rules about church attendance. One such conventicle, not far from Downton, was reported to the Bishop as meeting, illegally, every Sunday and Thursday *'at the Court House'* (which suggests a wealthy patron) and consisted of *'townes people and strangers and some Gentry, ye most meane people.'*

'SUFFERINGS'

'Sufferings' is a fair description of the savage fines and imprisonment they endured. These punishments were imposed even though the 1664 Conventicle Act and the Five Mile Act

of 1665, collectively known as the Clarendon Code, had the perverse effect of making it just legal for the first Baptist chapel in Downton to be founded in 1666 although any congregation of more than five remained illegal. The new congregation are said to have met in a cottage in Gravel Close where they later built the first chapel, probably on the site where the Downton Band now have their building.

Sanger lived until 1708. Initially, Downton Baptist church continued to grow, especially after the accession of William and Mary in 1688. It was considered to be the *'most wealthy and influential church of the General Baptists in the county.'* By 1699 however numbers had dropped to 13. At about this time Benjamin Miller became pastor and remained so for nearly fifty years, a time of new vigour.

It was a successful ministry and Miller also became Moderator of the General Assembly of General Baptists in 1709. Downton seems to have resisted also releasing him to be a Messenger who would go round other churches in the area to ginger them up.

SCHISM

In 1734 there was schism in Downton and some of the congregation began meeting in South Lane to *'preserve orthodox teaching'* and became Particular Baptists. They got support in the town and were joined by some local Presbyterians who had first joined the Baptist congregation at Broughton in Hampshire. Broughton thereafter took the secessionists under its wing. In 1791 they built a chapel in South Lane where the present one stands. The very first page of their Church Book is taken up with the application for and receipt of a licence from the Bishop of Salisbury - a reminder that, even 150 years on, nonconformists were not fully accepted. In 1801 they appointed their first minister so there was one chapel in Gravel Close and one in South Lane, perhaps 300 meters apart.

After Miller's death in 1743 the Gravel Close chapel had no minister for 15 years, relying on visiting preachers and leadership coming from Miller's son-in-law. Numbers dropped to 40 and it seems to have been an unhappy time. In 1777 some of Peter Coles' descendants who had control

of a large endowment left by a later Peter Coles withheld
the income and even the meeting place. *'A long and painful
state of darkness ensued.'*

NON-COMFORMISTS NOT CONFORMING

On a lighter note, the church elders may have been *nonconformist* as far
as the Church of England saw it but as the outside pressures and
sufferings decreased they became more and more concerned that their
own flock should themselves conform to the disciplines of the Baptist
ministry rather than the CofE. In October 1795 Rachel Dove reported to
them that Brother Mitchel, while returning from Salisbury Fair, *'did
make use of prophane language such as is inconsistent with his
profession as a follower of Christ'* Two months later a further charge of
the Brother's drunkenness was added by Rachel's husband, Richard
Dove.

When it all finally came before the church, Brother Mitchel was
accompanied by Brother Dove who himself stood accused of having
attended the Prayer Meeting *'disguized in liquor'*. Both confessed and
were restored but Brother Dove subsequently was accused of
drunkenness many times and as far apart as Salisbury, Wimborne and
finally on the Lymington-Poole road where he was caught by the
Lymington Baptist minister. This was in 1802 and he was accordingly
'cut off.'

OTHERS ARE CUT OFF

After years of attempted restoration, two men, Johnson and Shilly, were
also finally excluded. In that time they were variously accused of *'being
seen Breaking the Lord's Day in training a young horse to the neglect
of Divine worship'*; *'maliciously shooting his neighbour's dog...and
challenging him to a fight'*; playing cricket when there was preaching;
being in the company of an ungodly character; being *'an habitual liar
and deceiver'*; *'reveling'*; *'going to a horse race'*; gathering nuts on the
Lord's Day and, possibly the biggest and decisive error, failure to repay a
loan to a fellow member. Shilly's final misdemeanour was that, having
given himself up to a life of cursing and swearing, on a Saturday evening
*'he went to play the fidle to some dancers at Whiteparish. The Landlord
at a late hour turned them out and ... Shilly burst open the door and
continued in the house till one o'clock on Lord's Day morning.'* Too
much for the very forbearing brethren.

South Lane Church

The struggle continued until 1799 when the Court of Chancery gave judgement in favour of the church. £1,000 was invested and the interest from it to this day goes towards supporting the Baptist ministry in Downton. Numbers fluctuated but seem to have stayed around the 40 mark. In 1804 they joined the New Connexion of General Baptist Churches. By the end of the century they were reunited with their South Lane brethren although the Gravel Close chapel was still in use up to 1939.

OF A MIDDLING SORT

A final glimpse of this congregation in 1798 shows that, as in other parts of the south of England, a number of them were of *'the middling sort,'* papermakers, millers, maltsters, weavers, a chairmaker and a baker as well as several landowners. They accepted the discipline of their brethren. When one of the richest was accused of and admitted to fornication with his maid *'by which act she was pregnant prior to his marriage to her'* he was suspended. On being reinstated nine months later he asked to remain suspended longer in order to *'show to the sister churches and the world that he did not from his affluent circumstances influence the Church..'*

It was men of this sort who, in their thousands in Wellington's army, held great evangelical meetings on the hillsides by their camps. Fortescue, the historian of the Army, believed that it was their high morale that saved the Flanders army, eventually to confront Napoleon at Waterloo in 1815, from mutiny against the appalling conditions which negligence and incompetence in the War Office had caused. Whether any were from Downton has not emerged but it must be very likely.

Chapter 7

The Great Estates

LORDSHIP OF DOWNTON

The Bishops and the College had been benign and feudal landlords but they now divested much of their land to wealthy commoners. In the 17th and 18th Century it was these new landowners who shaped the countryside round Downton.

As early as 1551 the lordship of Downton manor was leased by the Bishop of Winchester to William Herbert. By 1621 the Herberts of Wilton, Earls of Pembroke, had also got the lease of Parsonage Manor from the College.

In effective control of the burgages and thus of the votes, the Earl nominated Edward Herbert as one of the Downton Members for Parliament. From this time Downton was a 'close Borough' for parliamentary purposes, in the hands of whoever was the principal landowner.

DOWNTON DEER PARKS

Barford Lane, a back way to Salisbury, is first mentioned in 1539 by that name although there are references to the road much earlier. Its original route is not entirely clear but it certainly did not go the way it does now. The first detour occurs just outside the village where the road turns sharply right, up the hill. This was to take it round Barford Park which had been enclosed by its owners, the Stockmans, as a deer park.

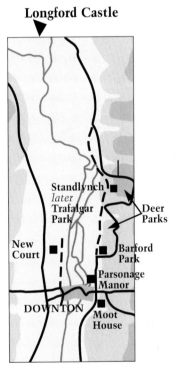

Newhouse is to the east of Downton

It makes another detour, again to go round a deer-park, at what is today Trafalgar Park but which in those days was Standlynch Park, owned by the Bocklands, maternal ancestors of the present Earl of Radnor. Standlynch was a rallying point for Royalists and, supposedly, Roman Catholics although the latter may just be political propaganda of the time. Large, comfortable houses had been built in both places and any cottages other than the farmhouses themselves were destroyed. Standlynch and Barford Park Farms alone remain of those settlements.

97

Moot House, earlier Downton House and/or Thrings, was the Manor House for the East Downton tything. It had been held by the Coles family from whom it descended to the Shuckburghs, already mentioned. The Coles later owned and upgraded Wick Farm.

New Court we have already discussed as the Bishop's manor house. The manor was leased from the Bishop at the end of the 17th Century by Sir Joseph Ashe and it was probably he who refurbished the present house. He was a benefactor of the village in many ways but in particular founded its first school. His reasons may have been enlightened self interest as he was seeking election as one of the two MPs and was causing very considerable and doubtless unpopular upheaval with his construction of water meadows both north and south of the Borough.

HOUSES AND HOVELS

The ostentation of the great country houses was in sharp contrast to the burgeoning rural poverty, especially in the south, where there was no alternative employment however menial. Driven out of their tied cottages belonging to the landowner for whom they had worked, many built hovels on common land, squatting where they could. No Man's Land was a whole settlement like this but even in Downton proper it happened.

Munday 16 May 1698

An account of those that in a riotous manner broke the Lady's waste within the Franchises of Downton by digging holes in the ground to putt posts for erecting a Cottage on the said waste.... and notwithstanding the workmen (whose names are hereunder) were forbidden by John Snow, servant to the Lady Ash, from proceeding any further in the said work, yett in contempt thereof they have proceeded and finished the said cottage.

Nicholas Lawes, senior, who is the owner of the Cottage, Samuel Wheeler, carpenter, Walter Sheppard, apprentice to Abr. Wheeler, Joseph Chalke, junior, who thatched the said Cottage, George Noble who breaded the walls of the said Cottage, one other man who holpe digge the holes for erecting the said Cottage.

This cottage may well have been completed in a single day - they often were. If you could get your house built, roofed, plastered and with a fire lit within the day on Common land you could claim ownership of the plot on which you had built.

THE GREAT LANDOWNERS

Four great families came to dominate the Downton area and, to a degree, the church: the Duncombes, the Eyres, the Pleydell-Bouveries and, later, the Nelsons.

As they now took over large sections of St Laurence's for their private use, as well as playing an important part in the life of the village, it is appropriate to look at them. Both the chancel, previously, possibly, the Bishop's chapel, and the South transept became for a time private chapels for the gentry. Their memorials remain as do faint traces of where the chancel partition stood.

BARFORD PARK IS BOUGHT

As a young man Sir Charles Duncombe was already lending money even to the King and in large amounts: £31,600 for just one loan, £50,000 for another, the equivalent to several million pounds as the Millennium ends. He became Receiver of Customs, Cashier of the Hearth Tax and a Commissioner of the Mint.

He was an active Member of Parliament and this may be why in 1690 he bought land and property in Downton. As a burgage borough the right to vote was vested in the properties he bought. He had just become an MP for Yarmouth in the Isle of Wight but Downton could be made the safest of safe seats by buying the burgages. By the time he died in 1711 he is thought to have owned three quarters of them. He had been MP for Downton, on and off, from 1695 till he died in 1711 revered and honoured by many, reviled by some.

In 1695 he had built Barford House in his newly fenced-in Barford Park. Sir Charles died in Teddington but is buried in Downton and his memorial is in the South Transept. He was unmarried so when he died his nephew Anthony inherited the Downton holdings.

Anthony Duncombe was only aged 16 on inheriting. He settled down in the great

Wattle before and after daubing and thatching

Barford House

house in about 1720 when he also bought the neighbouring Parsonage Farm, today called the Manor House. Next year he became one of New Sarum's MPs and held the seat until 1734 when he took over one of the Downton seats until he was made Lord Feversham in 1747.

In 1741 he had bought the lease of Downton Manor from the Bishop of Winchester. This gave him the right to appoint the returning officer so Downton was securely in his pocket.

The memorials in the chancel tell something of a life of tragedy. He was married for 40 years to Margaret Verney but by the time she died when he was 60, all their children had died. They were especially saddened by the death of George, the son and heir, aged 19. His memorial is eloquent. Lord Feversham's next wife, Frances Bathurst, from Clarendon Park, was only 25 when they married in 1756. She died after giving birth to a daughter, Frances, only a year later.

Margaret, Lady Feversham

Outside on the south chancel wall may be found:"This stone is erected in memory of William Kervil of . . .

A brief sum will show that he started work aged 11

In 1758 Anthony Duncombe married Anne Hales from Kent and she, too, was in her early 20's. They had a daughter they called Anne in the following year. He died in 1763 leaving his widow Anne with a daughter and stepdaughter. He is buried in St Laurence's with a fine memorial in the chancel.

BOUVERIES AND LONGFORD CASTLE

Up the road and river, towards Salisbury, on the next great estate, Edward, the son of Sir William Bouverie who had been Governor of the Bank of England when Sir Charles Duncombe was Lord Mayor, had bought Longford Castle and its land.

The Bouveries were Huguenot refugees who had left France for Amsterdam before the terrible St Bartholomew's Day massacres of August 1572 that all but exterminated the 400,000 Protestants still in France. The family came across to England, landing at Folkestone, and by maintaining their continental links were soon successful in London.

The castle had been built by Sir Thomas Gorges, c1590, in an unusual triangular form similar to those in Sweden that was the home of his Countess bride.

His cousin Sir Ferdinand Gorges was active in the exploration of America and was the first Governor of Maine in 1622. This was nearly 20 years after he had first become interested in Maine after meeting the explorer whose description of the East Coast of America was the trigger for its successful settlement. Lord Zouche not far away in North West Hampshire and the Earl of Southampton, Arundell, were working on a competing project, too, probably to create a safe haven for Roman Catholics.

THOMAS GORGES, HIS BRIDE AND HIS QUEEN

Helena Snakenborg was the daughter of a Swedish knight. She accompanied a royal visitor to the court of Queen Elizabeth I. She was only 16 and very beautiful when the elderly Marquess of Northampton fell head over heels in love with her. The Queen witheld permission for them to marry for a long time. Not long after they were married the Marquess died so Helena was back as a full time companion to the Queen, now as a Marchioness.

Five years later, in 1576, Thomas Gorges was dancing with her and tripped over her train and fell.

An account of what happened next is believed to be true:

'The next day he appeared in the royal presence with his right leg splendidly decked out and adorned. On the Queen asking why he made such a difference between his legs he said that his right leg had been honoured in such a way as he never could hope his left would - that during the faux pas of last night it had got between those of the beautiful Marchioness.

The Virgin Queen laughed out loud and bade him not despair as perhaps he might succeed in getting both his legs in the same position.'

He married Helena soon after and was promptly gaoled by the Queen for not getting Her permission! But all ended happily. It is said that the Queen gave Helena the proceeds of a rich prize following the Armada in 1588.

BOUVERIE AND DUNCOMBE JOINED

In 1765 Lord Feversham's widow, Lady Anne, now aged 29, married William Bouverie, 2nd Viscount Folkestone and, soon, 1st Earl of Radnor. This did not bring Bouverie the inherited Duncombe wealth that had mostly passed to a cousin in Yorkshire. However, the burgages and the lease of Downton manor were entailed in a complicated fashion to Lord Feversham and, more significantly, as he had an older daughter, Frances, to Lady Anne's 3 year old daughter Anne.

By a devious, costly but seemingly inevitable process the daughter, Anne, eventually became the next Countess Radnor when she married her step brother - and her inheritance ended up at Longford. The resulting quarrel with the Yorkshire Duncombe cousins dragged on for many years with the Bouveries and Duncombes frustrating each other's attempts to put Downton MPs of their choice in Parliament. For example, in the election of 1784 each side objected to virtually every vote cast for the other side and it took many months to sort out. The Bouverie line of argument was, generally, that Duncombe's bequest was invalid. The other side argued that Bouverie had improperly claimed burgage rights for property not in the Borough.

Thomas Duncombe Jnr.

BOBBY SHAFTO

Bonnie Bobby Shafto, famous from the song about his jilting a lover, had married an Anne Duncombe from the Yorkshire branch of the family. He lived in the Downton area and was Downton's MP from 1779 to 1790. Having been defeated by the Radnor candidates in 1790 and 1796, he sold his burgages to Lord Radnor, dying shortly afterwards. His wife, Anne, had three children in 1775, 76 and 77. She died in 1783 and was buried in Downton.

Their son inherited the Barford estate but seems to have had little interest in it. Barford House was taken down in 1815, perhaps after a fire. The Barford estate went to the Nelson family at neighbouring Trafalgar House in about 1835 and later to the Radnors.

DOWNTON AS A GIFT

Charles Shaw-Lefevre became one of Downton's two MPs in 1830. This is how it happened.

Scene: A gentleman's club in London. The elderly **Lord Radnor** is seated and has just put down his 'Morning Post' newspaper when he sees young Shaw-**Lefevre** standing in the doorway looking a little lost.

RADNOR: 'Ah, Lefevre. Just the chap. Hoped to see you soon. Come and join me.'

LEFEVRE: 'Good morning, Your Lordship. Thank you, Sir, it would be a pleasure.'

RADNOR: 'I've got a proposition for you. Just the thing. I'm sure you are the man for the job. How would you like to go into Parliament?'

LEFEVRE: 'Why, Sir, I would like that very much. Very much indeed.'

RADNOR: 'Capital. Capital. That's done then.'

LEFEVRE: 'Sir ?'

RADNOR: 'I have a seat for you in Wiltshire. Coming up soon. You will be most comfortable there, I'm sure.'

LEFEVRE: 'Well, Sir, I am very much obliged to you.....'

RADNOR: 'Don't mention it, dear boy. Don't mention it. How's your Uncle keeping these days? Haven't seen him in ages.'

LEFEVRE : 'Lord Eversley doesn't get out much these days - his old trouble, you know - still he has done pretty well, Sir, hasn't he? When should I go down to visit...?'

RADNOR: 'Visit? Visit? No, no, no. No need of that at all. The village is my affair. You do as you please in the Chamber, but this won't cost you a farthing. Leave it all to me.'

LEFEVRE: 'But, Sir...'

RADNOR: 'No buts. Do as you please and don't let them get a penny out of you. I must be off. Meeting in ten minutes. So glad we have settled everything so satisfactorily. Good bye, dear boy...'

LEFEVRE: 'Forgive me, Sir, I must insist....'

RADNOR: 'Yes, well, out with it lad...'

LEFEVRE: 'The name of the Borough, Sir ?'

RADNOR: 'The Borough! Good Heavens! What a noodle I am ... it's Downton, not far south of my place at Longford. You'll hear at the election and I'll see you in the House shortly...' He bustles off leaving a rather bemused young man who then turns to the audience and speaks

LEFEVRE: 'Of course the whole thing cannot be defended. I wasn't in the Commons very long - only a year. Then old Lord Eversley died and I was in the House of Lords. Still it was a very comfortable seat and Lord Radnor was as good as his word. I once had a request for money from the Vicar of Downton and the old Earl was very indignant as that was his affair, not mine. I always heard good reports of him, had a mind of his own....'

THE NELSONS OF TRAFALGAR HOUSE

We now turn to the family of Viscount Horatio Nelson, the victor at the Battle of Trafalgar. He was killed during the battle which historians see as the climax of a long and successful campaign at sea to contain Napoleon and which his contemporaries saw as a triumphal reversal of years of humiliation at hands of the French dictator.

A year after the battle a grateful nation had endowed the Nelson family with £90,000, [late 1990's value: £2,000,000] used to buy Standlynch House and estate under another Act of 1814, and a perpetual pension of £5,000 [£150,000p.a. today]. The Nelson Earldom passed to Thomas Bolton, the nephew of the first Earl, Nelson's elder brother William, and son of Nelson's sister Susannah.

Trafalgar House

Baroque Hall

Bolton changed his name to Nelson on succeeding. He was married to Frances Eyre who in turn was descended from Maurice Bockland and his wife, Joan Penruddock. The Nelsons, therefore, had family links with their new home that went back three and a half centuries.

STANDLYNCH HOUSE had been built for Sir Peter Vandeput, a wealthy banker, in 1733 to replace the semi-ruined manor house on lower ground near Standlynch Mill that had been there since the 14th Century. It is likely that the architect was Sir Peter's brother-in-law, Roger Morris, and his design was among the earliest in England reflecting the renewed interest in Greek architecture soon to be called Palladian. Morris was a great admirer of Inigo Jones and was assisting the Earl of Pembroke in designing the Palladian bridge at Wilton at the same time as he worked at Standlynch.

Vandeput's family like that of his neighbours, the Bouveries of Longford Castle, had fled from Catholic persecution of Protestants in Belgium and Holland by the Spanish Duke of Alva. The Bouveries were Huguenots and had earlier left France, before the terrible massacres of their brethren.

Standlynch Park was bought by Henry Dawkins, a dilettante, who had the designer, Revett, greatly enlarge and embellish it in 1766, building large wings to north and south connected by corridors to the main house and adding a magnificent Doric-pillared portico to Morris' original house. The wings were the work of John Wood the Younger, of Bath.

It was called Standlynch Park until it was bought by the Crown in 1815 for the family of Vice Admiral Viscount Horatio Nelson, the victor at Trafalgar. Under the Nelsons it was called Trafalgar Park and that is its name still today.

After a number of owners who hoped to find uses for the house it was bought by Mr Michael Wade whose family had built over 356 ships for the Royal Navy. A happy coincidence is that, when one of those ships, HMS GANGES, was sent by the Royal Navy to be broken up in the 1920s, Lord Nelson rescued some of the timber and had it used for panelling in the house.

Mr Wade's plans for the house include turning one derelict wing into an opera school but so far a viable compromise with English Heritage and other conservationists has not been found. Meanwhile the renovated parts of the house are being used for conferences, receptions and as a marvellous setting for films. Both 'Sense and Sensibility' and 'Emma' made use of this very handsome stately home. As the century ends a series of operas and musical events are bringing life again to a great but sadly neglected house.

THE LONG CONNECTION ENDS

The Nelson family retained Trafalgar House and over 3,000 acres until the middle of the 20th century when they too left.

In the 20th Century successive governments jibbed at continuing to pay the Nelsons their pension. They in their turn jibbed at not being allowed to sell the house or its estate that they claimed was costing them more than the pension! This was not resolved until a Labour government insisted and persisted.

In 1947 a special Act of Parliament amended the original 1806 Act so the pension stopped and the Nelsons were free to sell. The Duke of Leeds was the first buyer but he had soon sold on the bulk of the estate to the Earl of Radnor leaving Trafalgar House with 11 acres. The Duke had already let the house for 30 years to Lord Chandos, the former Oliver Lyttleton, who had had a distinguished career in Churchill's government. Lyttleton is best remembered for presiding over a great number of colonial independence negotiations as the British Empire evolved into the present day Commonwealth.

DOWNTON AND THE EARLS

We have not quite finished with these powerful families and their effect on Downton and its church. In 1791 the then Lord Radnor decided that, as it was in his Manor, he ought to be able to see Downton's church so he had an extra tier built in brick on to the tower of St Laurence's to achieve this. The construction was not a success. Remedial work needed between 1810 and 1815 to prevent the tower falling was not adequate and in 1859 the tower was reduced to its present, and original, size with only the four handsome stone pinnacles being re-used from the extension.

Having acquired the Lordship of the manor and the burgages, Lord Radnor was in dispute with the Bishop of Winchester over whether the Bishop's bailiff or the steward of the Lord of the Manor for the time being was the returning officer for elections. This was an important position in a Rotten or Pocket Borough like Downton where the owners of burgages would fill them with their friends and relatives just before and for no time after an election. Again Lord Radnor prevailed.

It was during this struggle that their respective owners ordered their numbers to be painted on the eligible houses. The only surviving example (no.16) can still be seen on Creel Cottage by Iron Bridge. A later form of marking can be seen on many houses in the Borough today. Set in to the walls are small stone panels with a number chased in to them. It is probable that this was done only to the houses owned by Lord Radnor and which in his view carried a vote. The rather capricious numbering is said to come from his Rent Book.

The old Pound

One of the houses no longer existed after the New Court Carrier was cut through but its right to vote lived on, marked just by the numbered stone visible from Moulds Bridge, or so it was said by Lord Feversham when speaking in the House of Lords during the Reform Bill debate.

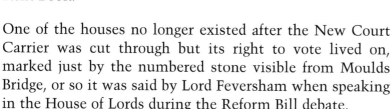

HAYWARD, STEWARD AND BAILIFF

Lords of Manors had many duties and, as many lived away, they delegated to paid subordinates. Some of these functionaries with legal duties were still being formally appointed as late as 1905. These days most of the work of a Steward is done by an Agent or Manager.

Mr George Futcher was Downton's last Hayward and Bailiff. He was Hayward from 1897 and Bailiff from 1905. His granddaughter still lives in Downton and she has provided some of his papers and his town crier's bell for safekeeping by the Downton Society.

HAYWARD The word derives from Old English *hege ward* or hedge keeper. His job goes back to Saxon times at least and he was an officer of the manorial court, duly sworn, serving the Lord of the Manor. Common meadows had many sharing them and each shareholder was responsible for a section of the communal hedge. The hedge kept the grazing animals from the equally important common arable land. The Hayward saw that the 'hedge' was kept intact. Often temporary hurdles or 'dead' hedges were used.

The Hayward's sanction was to impound stray animals. The pound in Downton was in the middle of the Borough more or less opposite the

Memorial Hall. Not an easy job as an entry for 1389 shows:

'If anyone's swine or porkers shall be so wild that they cannot be enclosed in the pound the hayward shall follow the animals to the house where they dwell and there by the view and testimony of the neighbours and trustworthy persons he or they shall have compensation according to the extent of the injury from him who claims the said swine'

Four hundred years later, in 1798, we find the customary charges for Hayward's Fees include:

'8. for impounding pigges that is rung fourpence each 4d

9. for impounding pigges that is not rung six shillings and eightpence each 6s 8d'

An unrung pig in a pound would do untold damage to meagre pasture with its snout in just one night so a charge twenty times as great was set and accepted. The same charges held in 1897. The pound was still in use in the 1950's when ponies and cattle from the New Forest strayed into the village much as they still do in Woodgreen, the other side of the cattle grids that now protect Downton.

Downton's Hayward had many other duties. He was the manorial official who saw tenants in and out, he supervised the elections of members of parliament, he was the Court and Town crier and was required to go to two market towns to cry *'straid horses cowes pigges and sheep.... imedetly after there entry'* He then had to keep them, if unclaimed, until the next Court Leet or his Lord would not be able to get his money - after a year and a day they were to be sold to *the best bedder to deffray expences.*

BAILIFF Initially *bailiff* and *steward* seem to have been largely interchangeable with the general inference that the bailiff was more in the legal chain and the steward more managerial but with considerable overlap. In Downton it was the Bailiff who decided the outcome of elections to Parliament but he was already subordinate to the Steward.

In 1905 Mr Futcher's duties were few. Chief among them was managing the *'Shows on the Green on Fair days'* where he was allowed to charge two shillings for a large stall and one for a small one. He must keep counterfoils (none to be torn out!); he could keep the money but must send the receipt book for annual verification.

His appointment came from a London firm of Solicitors who mention Mr Coxe as the Steward; the name of one of the partners in the firm was P H Coxe.

Chapter 8

Governing Downton

ELECTIONS TO PARLIAMENT

Election Day at the Borough Cross

Although Downton still had its two seats for Members of Parliament with an electoral roll of around 120 voters the electoral procedure had changed a lot since the 13th Century.

Elections were rumbustious affairs. They were held out in the open space on the Borough in front of the White Horse. Candidates or their agents ensured that the tenants of properties with burgage rights were there. They gave them their deeds as they went to the poll and collected them as they came away. 'Electoral roll' meant just that - the roll of parchment on which the electors were listed.

The voters would be well supplied with beer and waverers would be bribed as well. Technically, the right to vote went to a *'person having a freehold interest in burgage tenements held by a certain rent, fealty and suit of court of the Bishop of Winchester, who is Lord of the Borough, and paying reliefs on descent* [i.e. Death Duties!] *and fines on alienation.'* [a premium to the landlord when selling on]

When Parliament held a commission on what actually went on at elections they had several witnesses who cheerfully admitted to taking money from both sides - without fear or favour!

Burgage Numbers . . .

The election was managed by the returning officer. This was why it was so important to establish whether the Bishop's bailiff or Lord Radnor's steward held that office. He would stand on the balcony and call for a show of hands for each candidate. The heckling and general involvement of the crowd of voters and onlookers would at times be more like a riot. Name-calling and fights were usual and often the candidates had gangs of thugs to intimidate the undecided.

It was remarkable how different the count would appear to those looking out for the candidate's interest. Frequently, indeed during the late 18th and early 19th Centuries almost invariably, the election result would be challenged in Parliament. We saw earlier how family feuding between the Bouveries and Duncombes spilt over into election battles.

In 1832 places like Downton lost their burgage rights under the Reform Act. The then Lord Radnor, to his credit, backed the passing of the Bill that was to take away his powers. Even in 1900, 60 years after Downton's Rotten Borough status ended, we can find a rather disapproving comment in the Parish Magazine about a rowdier element's Election Day behaviour.

Note: Burgage Number and Street Number are different

LOCAL GOVERNMENT

Because Downton had been given to the bishopric of Winchester it was not subject to general royal taxes or administration. The Bishop or his bailiffs were the law. Effectively the Rector of Downton, after one was appointed, was the sheriff. The huge mediaeval parish was subdivided into six tithings: Downton, Church, Wick, Charlton, Bodenham and Witherington. 'Downton' contained Redlynch, Woodfalls, Warminster Green, Bohemia and Hamptworth. When the Borough was created it became a seventh administrative unit and was sometimes called Downton Foreign until the name finally settled as East Downton tithing.

There seem to have been three centres of government in Downton: the Courts of the Lords of the Manor, of the Borough and of the Parsonage under the Rector or Vicar. Each dealt with their own districts on behalf of the King. The Leet or local government for the whole parish was exercised in Tourns twice a year at which the Bishop's steward presided.

When the manor was leased the Lord Farmer's steward was in charge. By the 18th Century the name had changed from Hundred Tourns to Court Leets. Their function was to collect dues and deal with offences whether civil or criminal. Taverners and moral offenders and, later, Recusants [Roman Catholics who refused to go the parish church] and Dissenters were dealt with.

POLICING DOWNTON

From the early 17th Century a Constable or Hundred Constable for the whole parish was elected annually. He was assisted as a peace officer by the tithingmen who were also elected annually. In due course the tithingman or alderman for the Borough became the Mayor. There were other officers such as the searcher, the sealer and the registrar of leather. Most of these posts and the tourn ceased to have any other than ceremonial functions by 1842 when paid Parish Constables were introduced.

In 1816 the well-to-do citizenry were subscribing to the Downton Association which seems to have had as its main function the paying of rewards for 'information received.' There was a scale of rewards for different felonies.

Stealing from any Dwelling-house, Shop, Barn, or Buildings,—*Three Guineas.*

Feloniously stealing any thing where the Offence is not Capital,—*Two Guineas.*

Stealing any Waggon, Cart, Plough, Implement of Husbandry, or any Seed, Corn, or Grain thrashed or unthrashed, or any Staple Commodity.—*One Guinea.*

Stealing or destroying any Wood or Underwood; any Hurdles, Shores, Hedges, Poles, Rails, Posts, Fruit, Garden Tools, Turnips, Gardenstuff, Roots, or Vegetables; Milking Cows; Leasing in Corn Fields before the Corn is carried, without the owner's consent; or any other Offence,—*Ten Shillings and Sixpence.*

And if the Offender in any of the cases above mentioned shall be a Servant in the house of any Member of this Association, and have committed the offence against his Master or Mistress, in every such case,—*Double the above Rewards.*

Lastly.—That these Rules be publicly stuck up in every proper place in Downton, Standlynch, Bodenham, and Nunton; and that every Member of the Association have a printed Copy, with a List of the Society.

VILLAGE OFFICIALDOM

Many administrative functions, such as road maintenance, went to an increasingly centralised local government based in Salisbury.

Church affairs and much else in Downton were subject to the Churchwardens and Vestry. It was this body that, through its supplementary body the Select Vestry, was eventually to evolve into the Parish Council. The Vestry itself is now the Parochial Church Council.

The Mayor, with his mace, given by the town's MPs in 1714, remained in office for an obstinate 20 years more after the 1842 Act stripped him of any powers. So little of his powers remained in the early 1780s that there was a story current that if he saw three pigs wallowing in the mud on the Borough he had the right to whip up the middle one and lie in its place.

Authority for law and order vested in Justices of the Peace and in Coroners. Few of their early records have survived. Those that have give a picture of rural life with rural hazards in Downton in the 1750s and 60s. *'Mary Chalk: fell in to a pond and was drowned'*; *'John Miles, carter: killed by overturning a waggon loaded with wheat.' 'John Blake: fell under the wheel of a mill that was going and was immediately crushed to death.' 'John Cooper: killed by falling off a ladder'* are typical.

Slightly more unusual are: *'Roger Snelgrove: dropped down dead suddenly while putting on his clothes in a field where he had been at work'* and, last but not least, *'Mary Littlecot: had drunk too freely at the New Inn [in recent times, 'The Wooden Spoon'] and soon after was found dead'* possibly on her way home up the hill to Redlynch. Sadly, every so often the Coroner would record, as he did on 17 April 1778: *'George Weston: drowned himself; lunacy'* All suicides were put down to lunacy.

Most of the crimes were trivial with the occasional arraignment of women for infanticide although none from Downton were convicted. Quite a long and elaborate story of missing picks and shovels, accusations and denials, ended a couple of years later in 1736 with John Jennings being found with the tools stolen from William Jennings and Thomas Newman.

Sixty years later another Newman (there were plenty in the district) and George Quinton were executed in Salisbury for burglary after conviction at the Assizes. They seem to have mixed with a bad lot and confessed to receiving goods that could only have been stolen. They particularly regretted mixing with John Quinton who had led them in to stealing goods from a Mr Worral because John Quinton turned King's Evidence on them in order to escape the rope. After they had been hanged in Salisbury their friends conveyed their bodies to Downton for burial.

Elizabethan Judge on Circuit!

A much less drawn out affair comes straight off the page as alive as when it was written. Joan, wife of Joseph Davies, Downton tanner, reports to the Justices that *'this present day her said husband assaulted, beat and very much abused her in such manner that she is very much afraid he will take this opportunity to take away her life or do her some further bodily harm or mishiefe'* She evidently wasn't going to miss the opportunity given by the presence of the JPs.

'BOROUGH ENGLISH'

Over the centuries the Manor Courts had become ever more involved in the conveyance of holdings and settling disputes between neighbours, tenants and subtenants in addition to their revenue collecting and penal functions. By 1843, following all the changes in local government of the previous year, it could be said that the only practically useful business connected with any of the Courts at Downton was the conveyancing of copyholds of inheritance. This was serious business as the Borough tenancies and some others were 'Borough English'. That meant that the youngest son inherited unless some special reason or limitation could be shown. Courts for these transactions continued to be held in Court House until early in the 20th Century but their successors the Parish Council and the Parochial Church Council were very different both in character and in their powers.

16C Downton Burgess

POOR LAWS

Although there were problems from dispossessed vagrants setting up squatter villages on the marginal land in the parish - No Mans Land survives today as a reminder of them - there would have been few beggars and almost no actual starvation. England was way ahead of the rest of Europe with its Poor Law brought in by the Tudor kings.

The old Workhouse

In Downton the Poor Law would have been administered by the Overseers elected each year in the parish and it operated in two ways. Outside the close knit hierarchy of tenants and serfs and their families centred on the two manors who were looked after by their manor, the Poor Law provided shelter, food and clothing for the destitute and old and put to work those that were not part of the well ordered but tightly controlled system of the great estates.

Drunkards were put in the stocks. Vagrants and layabouts were sent to the House of Correction which evolved into the Workhouse. In 1723 ultimate responsibility was given to the Churchwardens and Vestry. Then in 1819 a body specifically charged with administering the new, much more detailed, Poor Laws was created. It was called the Select Vestry of which more later on.

Our Workhouse, built towards the end of the 16th Century, still survives but as a block of well-appointed flats at the top end of the Borough. It was next to the Smallpox House and incorporated the gaol. It had many uses over its long life and for forty years in the 20th Century was a bacon factory.

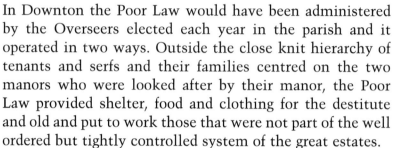
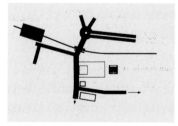

Chapter 9

Teaching Downton

SCHOOLS

In the early years of Winchester College the sons of parishioners of Downton were given preference - it is said that 10 of the original 70 places were reserved for Downton. This was a reasonable provision as so much of the College's revenue came from Downton, its first endowment by Bishop William of Wykeham.

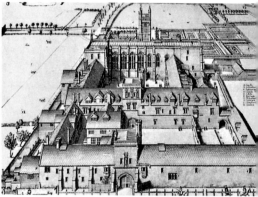

Winchester College

In 1679, Sir Joseph Ashe and Gyles Eyre of Brickworth, another wealthy local landlord whose family had made money in the Indies, established the Free School in Borough or Court House in South Lane for twelve boys. Court House had been built 4 years earlier. The boys should be sons of Borough freeholders but, failing that, they could just be living in the village. None could stay in the school for more than three years.

Eyre, who, like Ashe, was an MP for Downton, got permission from the King to start two Fairs (23rd April and 21st September) in Downton to fund the new school. Once the debts incurred by them in setting up the fair and the school had been cleared the income went to the school.

Court House

The first schoolmaster we hear of is John Sanger, the Baptist Minister, in 1645 and it is likely he was the master of the new school. The school was inadequately endowed with only £100 and the profits of the two fairs each year for which Gyles Eyre had got the royal licence. The Eyres were, at the very least, sympathetic to Dissenters at this time.

Much of the inspiration for Grammar Schools came from the attitudes that the Protestant revolution had fostered. In fact the school in Downton was notionally non-sectarian in choice of pupils.

Boundary Stone marker

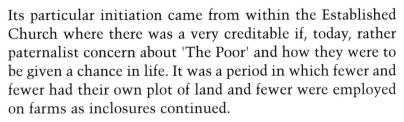

Its particular initiation came from within the Established Church where there was a very creditable if, today, rather paternalist concern about 'The Poor' and how they were to be given a chance in life. It was a period in which fewer and fewer had their own plot of land and fewer were employed on farms as inclosures continued.

The Free Grammar School survived in a poor way, never having enough income, until it was closed in 1890 despite having been enlarged by the vicar in 1833 and revived a little by a bequest in 1871. In 1801 it still only had 12 pupils.

Children's games

EXPANSION OF DOWNTON SCHOOLING

In 1784 Emma Noyes left £200 to be divided between paying for a schoolmistress in Charlton to teach 6 to 8 girls and the grammar school in East Downton. The latter was the only school in the village until the beginning of the 19th Century when there was a remarkable expansion in schooling. Some of these 'schools,' and there were 30 of them by 1820, were probably little more than sweatshops with between five and ten children being taught lace making but others would have given a smattering of genuine education.

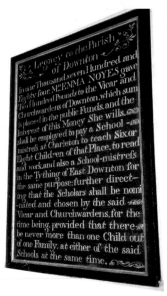

Emma Noyes bequest

The population was rising - from 2,450 in 1801 to 3,600 in 1831 - but employment was not. In 1801 John Britton, in *'Beauties of Wiltshire,'* wrote that *'the poor of this town* [Downton] *are principally employed in making lace.'* Inclosures, mechanisation and changes in crops and livestock management cut many youngsters off from their expected life as farm hands.

The evangelical, mainly nonconformist, churches were competing with the established pattern of Free or Grammar schooling managed or at least supervised by the Church of England. Evidently the Established Church did not feel that the multiplicity of small schools was adequate and in 1834 there is a report of a *'spacious schoolroom lately built by the present Incumbent Archdeacon Clarke near the church.'* Today this is the Church Hall. It is indeed spacious and one suspects was very cold and drafty when originally built.

In 1840 the British School was erected on land leased by Lord Radnor. It was built by the British and Foreign School Society to promote education with no affiliation to any particular denomination. It was for boys and was later converted into the Public Hall and then the Memorial Hall when the school moved out. It is used as the Election Polling Station when needed. In 1846 a similar school for girls was started in an old nonconformist chapel at the Headlands; today it is the Headlands Garage.

These were followed in 1847 by the National School in Barford Lane that was probably an enlargement of the spacious schoolroom built by Rev. Clarke.

Left: Primary School (ex-Board School)

Right: St Laurence Hall (ex-National School)

NATIONAL SCHOOLS were so called because they were set up by the National Society to *'educate the poor in the principles of the National Church.'*

BRITISH SCHOOLS were founded by the British and Foreign Bible Society, a non-denominational but highly evangelical and mission-oriented group.

BOARD SCHOOLS were established after the passing of the 1870 Education Act to be secular and independent of any religious orientation. Each community could form its own Board and then create a non-sectarian school for which it would get some Government finance. They were strongly opposed by both the Church of England and Nonconformists. One of the first boys in Downton to go to the new Board school had only to pay 1 penny a week.

CHURCH AND SCHOOL

There was a continuing wrangle in England between the Church of England and the Nonconformists over control of education.

In 1795 we find the trustees of the Free School in Downton telling the parents of its pupils that their children must be

presented to the Minister from time to time to be tested on their catechism. If they don't come up to standard then they will be expelled. So much for its original ecumenical intentions.

In 1823 the parish decided to withdraw its 40 boys (some evolution from the original 12) and their £20 per annum allowance. Finally in 1840 the school was put under the Diocesan Board of Education. Doubtless this was the trigger for the British and Foreign School Society's decision to provide an alternative British School in the same year.

The rivalry continued and in 1849 a National School was built in Barford Lane. No longer a school today (except for dancing and art) it is used as the St Laurence Church Hall - an example of how the life of the church and the life of the village are interwoven still.

In 1895 a Board School was built in Gravel Close. This was a secular school, much disliked by the Church. It was established to meet the requirements of the Board set up by the 1870 Educational Act and partly funded from London. Today, following the opening of the Secondary Modern School in the 1960s, it is occupied by the Church of England Primary School, moved from Barford Lane and under the same charitable foundation of 1847 which had built the Barford Lane National School.

EARL NELSON INTERVENES

It seems that the educational strife in Downton was particularly sharp. At the end of the 19th Century Lord Nelson wrote two long articles in the Parish Magazine justifying the educational arrangements that were so resented by the Nonconformists. It is somewhat contradictory to modern eyes but he both supported the dominance of schools by the Established Church and yet tried to persuade that the system was not unfair to Nonconformists. He was certainly trying to bridge the divide.

The first girls school . . . now a gagage

In 1904 as one of the first Bills of the new reforming Balfour Liberal government there was yet another Education Act but to judge from the protest march through the Borough in 1906 it still did not satisfy the free churches.

The first Sunday School in Downton was started on the Borough in a cottage just west of Mould's Bridge between 1789 and 1796, 200 years and more ago. It soon had to move up to the Church. By 1855 it had hundreds of children attending.

1906 Nonconformists' protest march

SCHOOL LOG ENTRIES

Jan 30 1891. Parents no longer pay a weekly amount for each child. During the severe weather boys from a distance (Redlynch, Charlton and Charford) have been allowed until 9.15 a.m. owing to the difficulty in walking.

June 20th 1891. Martin Witt has been removed by death and his name taken off the register. The attendance this week has been very poor owing to the number of boys at work.

June 30th. Four boys away at work. George Elliott being employed under-age.

July 4th. George Elliot still at work.

November 28th. The attendance this morning is very good considering the weather and the distance the boys had to come. [Some children walked five miles every day. One remembered, as a small boy, running home for lunch and running back, the distance being nearly two miles each way]

This afternoon, whilst at play, Annie Smith thought she spied a phantom beneath the roof of the porch. Her screams frightened many of the younger girls who began to imagine that they, too, were able to see spirit shapes. Their screams alerted me but it was not for a whole hour that the school was calm.

Dr Whiteley called at school this afternoon to complain of the children playing on the Barford Lane in the dinner hour. He had narrowly escaped running over Alice Lee; as it was she was quite under the horses. She cannot be blamed as she was returning to school. Dr Whiteley is driving a fast trap with rubber tires and NO bells. He turns corners with a great lack of care so that, should an accident occur, it should surprise no one.

Dr Whiteley came in to school this morning to complain that a boy had thrown a stone at his horse when he passed by yesterday. George Elliott was adjudged as the guilty boy and he was afterwards caned.

[Dr Whiteley's house and surgery were almost opposite the school in Hamilton House]

Chapter 10

Downton in Difficulty

A VILLAGE IN THE DOLDRUMS

Over the three centuries from the arrival of William and Mary in 1688 to the present, Downton has known little of prosperity and little of strife. Never a backwater it was never again an important place.

It was often a pioneering place, nevertheless. In 1740 a paper mill was built opposite the tannery probably by William Snelgar, a Salisbury papermaker. Samuel Snelgar was still there in 1769. In 1781 Joseph Jellyman had taken over and he was still there in 1803. It stayed in production until after the 1914-18 war. It specialised in handmade writing-paper. A second paper mill had a shorter life and later became the Downton Electric Light Company. It remained in service, generating electricity with water power, until the mid-1970s.

There had been a tannery in Downton in the 14th Century but it did not survive. However, it had certainly been revived by 1843, probably earlier (there were 3 tanners here in 1831), and a new tannery was built on the old site in 1919. It made high quality harness and saddle leather until 1998 when it finally closed, unable to beat lower priced competition while the English pound was artificially high in value.

Lace making was a cottage industry here until well in to the 20th Century. It had come over with the Huguenots. Children from the age of five would go to lace and reading schools. There is little doubt that this was exploitation of the worst, 'Water Babies,' kind. Lace making has survived, just, in Downton. Diana, Princess of Wales wore a garter of Downton lace at her wedding. This may have been the carrying on of a royal tradition going back hundreds of years.

121

DOWNTON TRADESMEN IN 1831

Bakers	7	Carpenters	25	Harness makers	2	Publicans	10
Basket makers	1	Cattle dealers	1	Iron founders	1	Sawyers	2
Blacksmiths	19	Coopers	4	Ironmongers	1	Shoemakers	21
Bricklayers	16	Corn dealers	1	Lime burners	2	Shopkeepers	15
Brickmakers	16	Fishmongers	1	Maltsters	4	Tailors	18
Broom makers	2	Glaziers	5	Millers	1	Tanners	3
Butchers	4	Glovers	4	Papermakers	5	Turners	2
Carriers	2	Grocers	1	Painters	1	Wheelwrights	9

This snapshot of Downton parish in 1831, already suffering from the loss of many cottage industries like spinning and weaving in face of industrial competition, gives a feel of a varied and thriving rural community but little to change its gradual relative decline in an age when Britain grew to its greatest wealth.

Maltsters producing the raw materials for beer-making reached their peak at the end of the 18th Century when four were producing 2000 quarters (close to 500 tons). In 1810 malting was 'carried on to a very considerable extent' and we can still find 4 maltsters listed in 1831. By the end of the 19th Century it had died out. One of the houses in High Street still carries the name of one of the maltsters.

Basket making by the Eastman and Rhodes families continued over nearly 200 years as did broom-making.

The Eastmans had been a wealthy and influential family in the 17th Century. Roger Eastman, born in Charlton but christened in St Laurence church in 1610, was an emigrant to Massachusetts in 1638. One of his descendants founded the Eastman Kodak company.

DOWNTON
VILLAGE
H·O·M·E·S

Midsummer Wood, Warren Copse, Woodgreen, Fordingbridge SP6 2QY
Tel: 01725 51255 *Fax:* 01725 512666

For prompt personal service telephone or call
01725 513777/510852

TRAFALGAR PARK

Ideal Location
for
Filming & Photography

Also available for product launches & special events

For further information please write to: The Manager, Trafalgar Park Limited,
Trafalgar Park, Downton, Nr Salisbury, Wiltshire SP5 3QR.

DOWNTON LACE

'The principal occupation of the poor in Downton is lace making.' So speaks a Trade Directory at the end of the 19th Century but in fact it was already declining fast.

Lace making had come to the south of England in 1550, brought by refugees from religious persecution in Europe. There are mentions of lace making in Salisbury in 1635. In 1698 there were 336 making lace in Downton, many of them children, so it is likely that Downton had had the industry for some time then. In 1752 Downton parish paid for two lace apprenticeships. These were long - eight to nine years - and demanding.

Lace making became so important a part of helping the poor that England banned lace imports from Europe, much to the annoyance of the French who banned imports of English woven wool!

In the early part of the 19th Century there was a sudden upsurge in lace making schools; Downton briefly had over 30. Notionally the girls were taught to read, write and do sums but in fact these were just sweatshops.

Making lace was done with a large pillow on the lap. Pins were placed according to the pattern in use. Then Downton bobbins loaded with cotton or linen thread were deftly interwoven to produce edgings or insertions.

Fashions changed and cheap lace could be made on machines. In 1851 there were 57 adult lace makers, in 1861 only 19 and, by the end of the century, very few indeed. Mrs Plumptre, the new Vicar's wife, was alarmed by the poverty of so many women in the village. In 1909, together with Mrs Robinson, she had collected over 500 patterns of lace, many of them unique to Downton. They started The Downton Lace Industry in what had been the Workhouse.

Sadly today there are only a few talented amateurs, no doubt earning a few bob from time to time, who keep this peculiarly Downton skill alive. Providing suitable lace for royal occasions was originally one of Mrs Plumptre's and Mrs Robinson's publicity stunts but it has become a Downton tradition much honoured in its observance.

BASKET MAKING

Willow withies were cut and collected from rented willow beds up and down the river from Downton. They were brought up in punts to Creel Cottage where they were sorted and kept underwater in bundles.

The bark was stripped off and the cruder baskets for apple picking were made from the bare rods. Finer work required the rods to be steamed in a huge copper vat. Eastmans produced furniture, baskets and hampers until after the First World War. Each weaver had his own designs and, inspired by continental examples, they produced intricate and lovely articles.

1839 Postmarks

ROYAL MAIL BRINGS A POST OFFICE

The first mention of a Post Office is in 1855 but there were ways of sending mail much earlier than this usually using the stagecoach or, for express and special delivery, carriers - riders carrying satchels of mail.

The first Postmaster General (by another name) was appointed in 1555 but the markings on letters from two hundred years earlier suggest government had a well organised postal relay system even then. The men who had the right to supply horses for those staging through had a duty to keep two horses available for carriers posting through with the mail.

One of the cross routes, dispersing mail from the main routes to and from London, ran from Marlborough to Ringwood. It is likely that The Bull, on the mail coach route would have been, in effect, the Post Office before the Royal Mail was formally created early in Queen Victoria's reign in 1840. However, there is no mention of a Postmaster in Downton in 1842 and the first Post Office was in the Square where the entrance to the old Tannery is now. Later the railway was to be the fast link with the outside world and for an extra charge a letter could be sent from any railway station to any other.

By 1870 the telegraph and telegrams were an even faster way of communicating and these, too, were operated by the Post Office until well after the 1939-45 war.

FARMING REMAINS IMPORTANT

Of course farming was still by far the biggest employer even though the 1831 table above does not directly show it.

Downton had been early in its use of water meadows. Inclosures had helped improve the quality of farming although many lost their livelihood as a result. This was especially hard after the end of the Napoleonic War in 1815 when there was an agricultural slump that was to last almost till the 1914-18 war driving many to seek emigration or a move to the towns. This slump was despite the Corn Laws that had imposed tariffs on imports and paid bounties on exports when prices were low at home. In effect England was running its own Common Agricultural Policy and it didn't work any better than the CAP of today.

The growing towns required more and more food so the big farmers survived. Then industrialists realised that if the import tariffs were abolished their workers would not be able to demand higher wages and Britain could insist that the tariffs imposed by other countries on imports of British manufactures should be stopped. By 1849 almost all import duties on food had been scrapped and cheap Canadian, American and Australian grain flooded in. Grain prices more than halved. Life was bad enough for farmworkers already but this was to trigger a further exodus to the Colonies and a new life.

The shepherd's work changed little . . .

NEW BREEDS, BETTER TRANSPORT, MECHANISATION

There were three main technical developments in agriculture during the 19th Century. The first was new strains of cattle, sheep and pigs to supply the greatly increased and prosperous population with meat.

A winnowing machine

The second was the improvement in transport. Roads and then railways enabled produce to be carried easily and cheaply. Downton did not get a railway until 1864 but it got the benefit of better communications long before then. A major help to farmers was the improvement of roads. This allowed them to move their produce speedily at low cost.

The third was mechanisation of farming. Drills, harrows, wheeled iron ploughs and later steam driven harvesting and threshing machines allowed English farming to compete to some extent although eventually the granaries of Australia and Canada and the USA would prove too much for many. Downton had its own inventor, Moses Boorn of Barford, who developed a new corn drill in 1789. Moses was also 'of Romsey' and as such was an Inclosure Commissioner for Charlton.

Farmers and their workers would come to the Church on Sundays, often twice. This was the place where much social activity took place. All were in their Sunday best. Gossip was exchanged, business done and romances started. Gentry and ordinary folk met if not as equals then very much as part of the same society. The churches for all their faults were the reason that England did not need a police force: Christian values and especially those of freedom of thought and of justice were the natural way for all.

INCLOSURES

Commons and Great Fields were a vital part of the cooperative farming brought by the Saxons. Commons usually were where the villagers grazed their cattle, sheep and horses. Some have survived to this day. Inclosure is the process by which such land held and worked collectively is divided into separate parcels. Owners give up their share of the collective rights in exchange for exclusive rights over their own plot. This carving up of common land had begun by the 13th Century although Downton, as one huge manorial estate dating back at least to Roman times, did not feel its effects in the same way as less tightly and centrally controlled areas.

In the early 16th Century the Crown became alarmed that inclosure by the major landowners would depopulate the countryside. Initially the impetus was to convert arable land into sheep runs. We have seen how this was managed in the Avon Valley by dividing the land into tithings that ran at right angles to the river up on to the hilltop pasture. The land here still remained in the ownership of the Bishops of Winchester although the form of leasehold they used meant that the tenants were seen in most ways to be the owners.

Between 1606 and 1801 there were a succession of private Inclosure Acts of Parliament. This was both to regulate inclosure and to give those who wanted inclosure the opportunity to constrain a minority of opponents. It was a slow and costly procedure that evolved into a fairly standard pattern.

Commissioners were appointed who made awards which were subsequently confirmed by a Court.

The 1801 Inclosure (Consolidation) Act codified the procedures for the future. To prevent corruption, or at least reduce it, Commissioners had to come from outside the area and were not allowed to buy land within it for five years. Maps were to be drawn showing boundaries and roads and responsibilities for consequential fencing of the awards - and, of course, fencing of land was the crucial point of the process. The maps can still be seen in Public Record Offices.

DOWNTON INCLOSURES

Inclosure of common land for private ownership changed the economy of the village dramatically. In Downton much that was not perhaps strictly inclosure because Common rights were not given up had already happened as the Avon Valley was given over to water-meadows. Three awards were made after the new procedure came in 1801, partly to confirm what had already happened.

In 1807 something over 10% of the land from Bodenham to New Court was apportioned with the biggest allotments going to the Earl of Radnor and his family (Pleydell-Bouverie), Henry Dawkins at Standlynch, and the Duncombes. 21 people shared another 150 acres - very small holdings even in those days. Indeed, in 1993 when the Inclosures were mentioned to a descendant of one of the 21 his fury at the injustice of what had been done to his family nearly 200 years earlier boiled over. Such memories may partly explain the village's reaction to proposals by those who benefited from the Commissioners' awards.

The Great Barn formerly at New Court and used to collect the tithes

In 1822 another 2150 acres were allotted in East Downton and Hamptworth Manor. In Downton there were 94 allotments so it was a complicated division but the Pleydell-Bouveries had something over 900 acres, the Duncombes (or, rather, Bobby Shafto) perhaps 700 acres and the Eyres of Newhouse also were awarded a sizeable acreage. In 1847 came the last of these Inclosures, in Wick tithing, in which 959 acres were inclosed in 8 allotments. The Earl of Radnor received more than 500 acres, George and Harriet Matcham were allocated over 200 acres. George

The Trenching gouge
ube vsed as the
Spade

The Turving
Spade

The Trenching
Spade

The
paring Spade

The Trenching
Wheele plough

The plaine Trenching
Plough

Fig 67

The Single
Wheele plough

The Trenching
Spade Cutting
t's trench &
he Water
ollowing

*Tools and skills
outmoded*

was Admiral Nelson's nephew and she was the Eyres of Newhouse's heiress.

Other names that have figured in one or both of the earlier Inclosure Allotments and which recur here are Baily, Moody, Taunton and Whitchurch. The Bailys were farmers at Wick but seem to have had extensive if small holdings elsewhere. The Tauntons farmed in Redlynch and they and the Whitchurch family were Baptists.

It was the tragedy of the inclosures that the independence and freedom of the generality of country people could not survive once their casual labour was no longer needed and their common land had been taken. In 1831 the Minutes of the Select Vestry [Parish Council today] talk of 100 men 'out of employ' in the winter months and from 30 to 40 at other times.

POOR AND UNEMPLOYED

Looking after the poor had been a continuing part of the parishioners' duty to their less favoured fellows. Parliament was very aware of the dangers of a dispossessed mob and there was a steady flow of measures to make sure parishes looked after all their people. We have seen how the Overseers of the Workhouse were elected. Downton was a member of the Alderbury Union: groups of parishes sharing the burden of looking after their poor, sick and old.

In 1723 the Vestry (Parochial Church Council today) was given oversight of Churchwardens and Overseers in their provision of housing and employment of the poor. In 1819 this was strengthened by the so-called Select Vestry of 'substantial householders and occupiers of land.' Downton immediately formed one and it reads like a Who's Who of the village. Headed by the parson, it included Earl Radnor, Earl Nelson, Bobby Shafto's son and near a dozen others.

Its Minute Book makes interesting reading. Vaccination against smallpox, closing noisy pubs on Sunday evenings, a form of community service to get back for the village in work some of the cost of housing and feeding the unemployed, organising lighting and a watch for the village, measures to combat cholera and so on.

Some of the decisions were about personal supplies to inmates: *'Harriet King applies for a bed blanket and coverlid (she being very ill) - granted.' 'James Armney was committed to the House of Correction for 3 months hard labour, as a rogue and vagabond for leaving his wife and family chargeable to this parish - the sum paid to his wife was £7, none of which he repaid'*.

There were arrangements to borrow money to pay the expenses of any who wished to emigrate to Canada and meetings to explain to would-be emigrants what would happen. This was local government at its best, responding to central government advice to meet the actual needs of the village.

The reason why emigration seemed such a good idea was that Downton had been through a particularly bad patch. Harvests had been poor for the three years from 1828 to 1830. The mechanisation of threshing had led to riots in many parishes and the government reacted harshly. 153 were tried and deported to Australia although as far as is known none were from Downton.

In 1831 the Select Vestry decided it wanted more effective work from those to whom it was giving the dole as well as recognising how morally debilitating the existing system was for the poor. In effect those on the dole were allotted to work for those who were providing the poor relief funds rather than having work provided by the Parish. They were paid 9 shillings a week which was a subsistence wage for a small family.

Then, in 1832, cholera came to Downton and a bad situation became disastrous with breadwinners dead or unemployed and the village unable to maintain its poor.

In 1835, Samuel Payne, Assistant Overseer of Downton Parish describes the unemployment problem thus:

'Prior to the winter of 1831 the superfluous labourers of this Parish were generally employed on the roads or in the gravel pits in congregated masses of from 50 to 100, the few industrious Labourers being thus brought into contact with the indolent, dishonest and profligate, the former

'Punch' took a wry look at emigrants.

Ticket Clerk has just taken emigrant's passage money.

'What about your trunk?'

'What would I do with a trunk?'

'Well, put your clothes in it?'

'What! and me go naked!'

then assumed the character of the latter, and theft rioting drunkeness became the result.....

In consequence of which the Churchwardens and overseers finding it absolutely impossible to conduct Parochial affairs under such circumstances...'

CHOLERA MORBUS HITS DOWNTON

In February 1832 the Select Vestry called a general meeting of all the inhabitants to brief the population on coping with cholera. Provision was made for a temporary hospital in the Borough (possibly supplementing one already in existence at the junction of Lode Hill and Slab Lane although so far this hospital's establishment has not been confirmed).

- Help with food, fuel, clothing and bedding was organised.
- The cottages in the Borough were to be whitewashed.
- Gravel was to be supplied to fill the 'useless drains and other holes in which water and mud have been left to stagnate.'
- Inhabitants were to 'remove from their dwellings filth of every description, particularly dung and ashes; to cleanse their drains and privies and to burn all decayed articles of rubbish such as rags, papers and old clothes.' If it was not done then a team of men was to do it anyway.

There follows a Memorandum listing 'articles recommended as particularly useful at this time.'

- Comfortable straw or chaff beds with extra blankets.
- Bags to hold hot bran, sand, ashes, corn, or salt.
- Flannel shirts with large loose sleeves and large flannel night caps to be worn by the sick.
- In case of death, the corpse not to be washed nor carried at burial into the church.
- The coffin to be carefully pitched in the inside (and whitewashed on the outside).

220 EMIGRATE TO CANADA

It was to remedy this that the Special Vestry in Downton, like those in many other places, sponsored the emigration of 25 paupers from Downton to the Talbot Settlement in Ontario and they took ship from Portsmouth in May 1835. Those chosen seem to have been hardworking and enterprising and their reports home were so positive that

The emigrants leave for Portsmouth

there was no difficulty in recruiting a very much larger group to take passage the following year.

In 1836 we find the following in the Select Vestry Minutes dated 27th February: *It was ordered that a notice be given in the church tomorrow for all fathers of families and all single persons that wish to emigrate to Canada are to attend a meeting of the Vestry on Monday next at three o'clock in the afternoon in order to have their names entered for the purpose of securing their sea passage and other necessary arrangements.*

TALBOT'S MIGRATION

Colonel Talbot had returned from his job as secretary to the Governor of British North America, Simcoe, to fight in France. In 1803 he sold his commission and emigrated to Canada. There he contracted with the government *'that 200 acres be allotted to him for every family he shall establish thereon. 50 acres to be theirs for perpetuity and the remaining 150 acres of each lot to become his property, for the expense and trouble of collecting and locating them'.* This land was reserved for him along the shores of Lake Erie and he is said to have settled 40,000 under this scheme. His scheme would have been going for upwards of 30 years by the time the Downton parties arrived.

Although there are no further references in that book, Alderbury Union records note that a *Mr Hammings as Guardian of the Parish of Downton applied for 25 pairs of men's shoes, to lace; 100 girls' and boys' shoes from 3 years*

THE 3RD EARL RADNOR, THE BATTLE OF PYT HOUSE AND DOWNTON EMIGRATION

While the first and second Earls of Radnor seem to have been primarily concerned with acquiring and holding the great estate that is still held by the family today the third Earl had much wider interests. As Viscount Folkestone, before he inherited the Earldom, he was a Radical Whig MP sometimes for Downton but mainly for Sarum (Salisbury) for over 20 years.

Not long after he had become the Earl he was involved as the Chairman of the Bench of Magistrates in dealing with the Pyt House riot. This was one of a series known as the Captain Swing riots which spread across the whole of southern England in the last quarter of 1830. Bad harvests, low wages, unfair game laws and, the final straw, the use of threshing machines that deprived men of their winter work caused resentment to boil over in a wave of destruction of machinery and property. The Battle of Pyt House was at Tisbury, west of Salisbury, at the home of an MP called John Bennett and it was the most serious of the whole series.

One man was shot and killed when 40 mounted and armed men of the local militia confronted a mob of several hundred men. 29 men were arrested and taken to Fisherton Gaol in Salisbury. They were examined by magistrates and employers and others spoke out for many of them. A number were released, discharged with a caution.

Lord Radnor as Chairman of the Bench told them they should, in future, bring their grievances to the notice of magistrates in a proper manner when they could be redressed. 17 of the men went forward to trial at a Special Commission of Assize. 16 were convicted and 14 were condemned to either 7 or 14 years transportation to Australia. One went to New South Wales and the rest to Hobart in Tasmania. None returned but one who somehow evaded arrest lived fairly openly at home, hiding when anyone in authority passed by.

That Lord Radnor should be directly involved in the emigration from Downton to Canada by both guaranteeing the government loan of £1,000 and paying the interest may well partly stem from this experience of how desperate very moderate worthy men could become when their families starved. In any case the village could not carry the burden of poor relief indefinitely and this way those who stayed and those who went both benefited.

In 1830 Lord Radnor was insisting that the two men he nominated as MP's for Downton should support the new Whig Government's plan for constitutional reform that were, in 1832 to disenfranchise Downton, his Pocket Borough: too little is known of this liberal and open-minded man.

Pyt House riot

old to fifteen; and 25 pair of women's shoes for the use of the Poor about to Emigrate from Downton Parish. The clerk was to order them from London. So that makes at least 220 men, women and children who had been shipped out of Downton in two years, many of them in a ship chartered for £1,300 by the Select Vestry.

Lord Radnor undertook to pay the interest on the loan of this money by the Government. He, like other major landowners, would have been a major contributor to the Poor Relief that would now no longer be required for those who left the village. This exodus was a sizeable proportion of the total population, not far short of 10%, and probably included most of those permanently unemployed who were fit enough to go.

The Vicar of Downton received a number of letters from happy migrants . . .

Downton's 1836 project was reported to Parliament as the biggest in Britain for that year.

In 1861, three were helped to emigrate to Australia. The modern city of Adelaide in South Australia has at its heart the settlement created by rather more altruistic men than Talbot but most of them did not even trouble to visit the place they were sending thousands to pioneer! Thomas Poulton, 18, was one of them. We may never know how many left Downton during those difficult years - currently we know of about 220 - but occasionally their descendants call by.

to do, that I can earn from a dollar to ten shillings a day. You told me that we should repent of coming to Canada, and surely we do, but it is because that we did not come before. This I have to say, that any labouring man can live better by working three days a week than at home by working all the week. But should any think of coming, I would first advise them to lay it to heart whether they can wean their hearts from the old country first, not to reflect after. Many were so weak-minded as to think that we were going to be sold as slaves. But I can certify, that this is the place for liberty. Here are no poor-rates, for there are no poor here. There is plenty of deer and wild turkeys, and pheasants and game, free for any one. But I don't trouble about it at present, for it pays me better to get to work, but there are many that do.
Please to tell Mrs. Roberts that if they were here, she could get a plenty of places for her girls. They are very much attached to English girls, and get a dollar a week for them.—Please to tell Wm. Chalk that brick-making is good here.—Should any think of coming, tell them to come away by the beginning of March, as they will have the summer before them. But as to the state of the country, it is a fine country, and very healthy.—Lace sells well here. Tell any

PUBLIC SERVICES

The Select Vestry involved itself in every aspect of village life as we saw from extracts from their Minutes. Many services we now take for granted started in a small way with their intervention. Some of them are picked out below. The Select Vestry was replaced by the Parish Council in 1895.

LAW AND ORDER

The evolution of policing Downton since 1832 has verged at times on the revolutionary. The change from the local Bobby (deriving his name from Sir Robert Peel) living in the village and perfectly willing and able to lift two misbehaving youths one in each hand and bang their heads together to today's mobile but largely impersonal technocracy would be incomprehensible and even frightening to earlier generations.

Punch thought we would get better policemen if we paid them more . . .

For the record, Downton's policing at the end of the Millennium is based at Alderbury, three miles north of Downton, which in turn comes under Salisbury. The Alderbury 'patch' covers 22 villages in 80 square miles containing 16,000 people. The work is done by 7 uniformed officers, one detective and one plainclothes officer all under the control of a Sergeant. Highly mobile, computor-assisted and with excellent communications they are as abreast the times as any section of the community - we just don't see them until there is trouble!

Inevitably the modern police reflect their times. Some years ago it was known that some IRA men were operating in Southern England. A local landlady reported to the police that two of her overnight guests were acting suspiciously. She thought they might be Irish. They had gone across to The Bull where they now were....

Almost before she could put the phone down, the village was full of police cars and armed policemen. Two young men were legging it out of the back of the pub and over the wall only to be intercepted. Not Irish Republican Army - just a couple of welchers avoiding paying for their overnight stay....

STREET LIGHTING

In 1831 street lighting was provided. These were oil lamps using oil supplied, latterly, by Dunmore, the chemist. There was, of course, a lamplighter. Before the 1914-18 war he was John Godwin. He was paid one shilling and sixpence per night. In 1913 the Parish Council is reported as considering acetylene for street lighting. It is not until 1921 that they dispose of their lamp oil tank. The year before that, they had applied for a grant of £650 from the County Council *'to provide an electric cable in order to light street lamps.'* As with the change to gas, this may not have gone through because, in 1928, we find the Rural District Council and Viscount Folkestone agreeing to the Tanning Company, who owned the hydroelectric plant, running a temporary cable from there to the Headlands for a number of street lights.

Today there are many more lights and they are the responsibility of the Council.

GAS AND ELECTRICITY

Various attempts to supply petrol and acetylene gas from what is now Green Lane were not successful for any length of time. Since 1990 there has been a mains gas supply through most of the village. Electricity was supplied by the hydroelectric plant from 1935 to 1972. Today the whole village is supplied with electricity from the National Grid.

REFUSE

Some attempt was made during the 1832 cholera epidemic to improve refuse disposal but it was not until 1928 that a weekly collection by Mr W Barrow was started. One man, one horse, one cart cost the Parish eleven shillings a week with another five shillings and sixpence if an extra man was needed.

Today's collections, spread over several days (although still weekly for householders), show yet another part of the revolution in our way of living in this century.

WATER AND DRAINAGE

The water-carrier supplied Lode Hill

Cholera in the 19th Century made the British very water and drainage conscious but in Downton, except during the epidemic, little changed. Most houses had their own well although some only had use of a communal one. Down on the river flood-plain water was easy to find. Houses only needed a 'crook and bucket' to draw water but many had a hand- or, later, an electric-pump.

In 1952 the West Hants Water Co. laid freshwater mains through the village but before that the Tannery owned a well on Lode Hill that gave a limited supply. Water was pumped by hand by workers from the Tannery and piped to taps on the Borough Green. When this was insufficient for local demand the supply was discontinued and this may have triggered the arrival of a proper water supply.

Earth closets at the end of the garden were usual although anyone close to running water - the river, carrier, bunny or drain - was apt to use this with the facilities hanging over the water. A canoeist coming down the Avon in 1939 remembered the breezy arrangements at one welcoming riverside cottage.

In 1884 the Vestry memorialised the Highways Board [County Council] to the effect that most of the owners of property in Downton High Street would be willing to cooperate in laying pipes and laying drains because the drain on the South side of High Street was a continual source of danger to passers-by who were likely to fall into it and was also a nuisance from the sanitary point of view. The work was done and 'many of the houses in High Street were connected to a drain which ran down to the river'.......!

Mains drainage was not completed in Downton for a further 75 years. Outlying houses are still dependent on the cesspit and its successors.

Chapter 11

Worship Changes

METHODISTS AND OTHERS

John Wesley's astonishing lifetime ministry, riding from meeting to meeting on horseback across the country well in to his nineties, is thought by some to have saved England from bloody revolution. Records for Downton's Methodists are scanty but in 1814 a new chapel was built and in 1815 the Sunday School opened. This coincided with the end of the Napoleonic War and it could be that returning soldiers, converted while in the Army, as so many were, formed and organised the first Wesleyan Methodist Congregation here.

1884 Methodist Chapel

Whether there was an earlier congregation we do not know but in 1827 Sarah Nicholas joined a Methodist Society in Downton having been in the *Wesleyan* Sunday School. This may imply that there were already two Methodist meetings in the village. We know that they were well attended although a figure of 29 members in 1823 gives an interesting measure of the comment that Downton was then *'one of the most flourishing Methodist societies.'*

In 1849 there was a breakaway of part of the congregation to form the Downton Reform Church. The original chapel fell in to decline and was closed in 1919. There had also been Methodist meetings in what was earlier the Cottage Hospital and later the butcher's shop [on the corner of Slab Lane and Lode Hill] and that congregation may also have moved to the Reform Church.

To begin with the new group met in a small thatched cottage but numbers grew rapidly and the headmaster of the British School let them use two cottages he owned in High Street. This was where the present chapel was eventually built in 1884. Building became possible after he died and the land had been made over to them.

The new chapel was so well attended when first opened that the elders had to pack people in to the pews. Even that was not enough and, ten years later, a further sixty seats were created by building a new rear wall and extension towards the High Street. That is what we now see from the High Street.

The congregation changed their name to United Free Methodists and linked up with a like-minded church in Milford Street, Salisbury. It is they alone, with a small and largely elderly congregation, valiantly struggling to maintain the traditions, who survive today in Downton.

> **In 1865 the non-conformist churches were:**
> **Baptist New Church, South Lane**
> **Reheboth (Baptist), Lode Hill**
> **Wesleyan (Conference), near the Tannery**
> **Methodist (United Free) andWesleyan (Reformed), High Street**

REHEBOTH BAPTISTS

Reheboth chapel, now a garage.

John baptises Jesus

We saw earlier how the Baptists had difficulty in remaining united and in 1842 there was a new rift. This resulted in a small congregation gathering on Lode Hill. Their founder was a fiery orator called Tiptaft but known locally as the Thunderer. On one occasion he was conducting a full immersion baptism in the river watched by a jeering, hostile crowd. A stone was thrown.

The Thunderer turned on the crowd and in a great bellow quoted the biblical verse: *"Be not deceived, God is not mocked; whatsoever a man soweth that shall he also reap."*

They later had a pastor called Janes. After he died in 1858 the congregation seems to have ebbed away and he was not replaced. Today the chapel is a private garage.

ROMAN CATHOLICISM RETURNS

After the terrible years under Queen Mary (1553-1558) when many brave Protestant Englishmen were martyred for holding to their beliefs, the English were slow to accept Catholics back in to public life and, at times, Catholics were actively persecuted.

In the 19th Century the external political threat from Catholic kings had disappeared. Nonconformists were ever more restive under the constraints on their freedom still insisted on by the Established Church and they were getting ever more powerful politically. Many of the great entrepreneurs of the Victorian period belonged to various of the Free Churches.

Gradually, gradually more and more concessions were made. At last, in 1871, there was no longer any legal barrier left to public office for Catholic or Dissenter alike. This political change in England happened to coincide with a defiantly assertive and aggressive revival of Catholicism world-wide.

DOWNTON'S CATHOLICS

Through 300 years Catholics had gathered more or less secretly at Odstock Manor and later at Arundell House in the Close in Salisbury. Those who would not acknowledge or attend the Church of England were known as Recusants. In 1783 the resident curate in Downton reported to his Bishop that there were only a few poor and old Recusants in his Parish although since 1778 it had no longer been illegal to practise the Catholic religion.

An important Catholic convert in Downton was Countess Nelson although her husband, the third Earl, remained loyal to the Church of England. She died in 1904 but it was not until the Earl died in 1913 that her family were free to return the Standlynch chapel in their grounds to Catholic usages.

They continued to support Catholicism in Downton and in 1939 the Catholics built a house for a Catholic priest on land given by the Nelsons. This was along Barford Lane between the chapel and the village and was known as The Bungalow. Its single attic room was said to have been the priest's private chapel.

At some stage during or immediately after World War II the priest left and the house was let. It was only in 1978 that the Catholic hierarchy finally gave up the idea that they would return and the house was sold into private hands.

St. Laurence tower raised . . .

When the Nelsons knew they were to be allowed to sell and leave their Trafalgar estate and that the chapel would belong to new, probably non-Catholic owners, they gave a plot of land on the northern edge of the village. There, in 1950, the Bishop consecrated a Chapel of Ease dedicated to 'The Good Shepherd and Our Blessed Lady Queen of Angels.' The large icon in it came from the Standlynch chapel. This chapel is in active use as the Millennium ends, served by the Salisbury parish priests and with upwards of fifty attending.

It is a measure of how far things have changed that the Churches Together in Downton can include the Catholic chapel as a venue for ecumenical services for joint acts of Christian worship.

ST LAURENCE TOWER LOWERED

In 1860 St Laurence's Church had a major uplift, if such a term can be used about the depredations of T H Wyatt and D Brandon.

It was triggered particularly by the need to save the tower from collapse by removing the extra layer built in 1791. This had been causing problems by 1810 when a previous phase of remedial work, including the restructuring of the western arch at the crossing, was carried through.

. . . St. Laurence tower lowered

It is just possible that the final straw was the addition in 1856 of two more bells to the four already there; equally it may be that it was the decision to add the bells that precipitated the restoration or it may all have been one operation.

Happily the stone Georgian pinnacles and battlements which had topped the extra stage were kept for the reduced tower. T H Wyatt was a nephew of the Wyatt who devastated Salisbury Cathedral in the previous century. He was quite a competent as well as a popular architect but was imbued with contemporary views of what churches should be like with seriously destructive consequences for the old church.

DANIEL ALEXANDER AND DOWNTON CHURCH

In 1810 Lord Radnor was carrying out massive alterations to Longford Castle. Wyatt had produced plans for its conversion but in the event Daniel Alexander was employed. They were extremely costly - nearly £6,000 in one year alone [which would be at least £1,000,000 today] - and very slow. Relationships seem to have remained friendly.

In 1810 Alexander made four visits to St Laurence church to assess the damage being caused by the heightened tower. At the end of his report he remarks: *'Mr Lear wished me to give some estimates but I would not enter in to that.'* There is a postscript to Lord Radnor saying: *'This matter gave me much pleasure to do therefore I beg leave to decline my charge.'*

Between 1812 and 1814 the 2nd Earl paid for repairs to the church. The bills tell their own story.

> *1812 James and William Croone, Masons. West arch of tower £116.10s.2d*
> *1814 William Pope, carpenter £17.17s.2d*
> *Thomas Snelgrove, bricklayer £3. 9s.5d*
> *John Humby, smiths work £4. 4s.6d*
> *James and William Croone, masons £4.17s.4d*
> *Joachim Hibberd, plaisterers work £17. 3s.8d*
> *1815 Joachim Hibberd, plaisterers work £25.17s.7d*

Finally in 1818 Daniel Alexander is paid £25 for his site visits @ three guineas and to see Rev. Lear @ two guineas plus commission on the works.

Sadly Wyatt did not deign to leave a record of what he found and then destroyed. We know that there was a partition between the chancel and the eastern end of the crossing. This is believed to have had a doorway in it leading through to the chancel which may first have been the Bishop's private chapel. Much later it became the Duncombe mausoleum and, perhaps, their chapel, too. Wyatt removed it.

The interior was stripped of ceilings, panelling (the chancel was oak panelled), and most of the furnishings. Some of the chancel panelling survives at Newhouse. The sounding board for the old pulpit is now used as a table in the vestry. The Ten Commandments painted at the top of the nave probably date from the time of Wyatt's work. The organ was made in Bath by Sweetland in 1870. It is a two manual

instrument with 8 Great and 7 Swell stops and the 'usual pedals and couples.' It is in need of a major refurbishment.

Little has changed in the appearance of the church since. We have been left with a simple and elegant and evocative structure. It speaks to us in dozens of little ways of the continuing faith of our ancestors expressed differently in each generation.

Outside in the churchyard the 13th Century stone cross is probably now our only visible link with those buried outside who in earliest times worshipped inside. The weathered stone grave memorials are a more immediate link with the past. The War Memorial in the North aisle, showing the awful cost of war, reminds us that this is the village church for all its people

BELLS

In the church tower there is a peal of 8 bells and a Sanctus bell.

Oddly, the Sanctus, the most recently hung, in 1998, is also the oldest. This bell has no inscription but had hung for 500 years in St Swithun's Church, Patney, Wilts before its church was made redundant and demolished. It is believed to have been made around 1400. It was dedicated by the Bishop of Salisbury on 8th April 1998 and named PATNEY ST. SWITHUN.

The Sanctus bell is static, hanging from a frame. When it is rung during the high moments of the Communion service the clapper is pulled sharply against the bell.

For the ring of 8 bells the arrangement for change ringing them is that found almost uniquely in Britain and almost never found in Europe.

Each bell in its rest position is upside down. The bell rope goes round the outside of a large wheel and the bell ringer frees the bell to swing down and then with a great heave gets his or her bell to swing through almost 360 degrees up to the top again where it is held till next wanted. The clapper strikes the swinging bell in its orbit with far more force and freedom than if just pulled against the bell. This is what gives English bell-ringing its distinctive sound. To even the wear, bells are turned from time to time so that the clapper strikes a fresh part of the bell.

BELL INSCRIPTIONS

No 1: 1939-1945 TO THE GLORY OF GOD AND IN GRATEFUL MEMORY OF THE MEN WHO LAID DOWN THEIR LIVES. M. & S. LONDON 1946

No 2: 1939-1945 SOUND OUT THE BELLS, IN GOD REJOICE. M.&S. LONDON 1946

No 3: C&G MEARS FOUNDERS LONDON 1856

No 4: SAMUELL KNIGHT OF READING MADE MEE 1692

No 5: [ca.1450]+ O SANCTE IHOHANNES

No 6: PRAYSE YE THE LORD I W 1604

No 7: C&G MEARS FOUNDERS 1856

No 8: [Originally 1713] CLEMENT TOSIER CAST ME IN THE 12 YER OF QUIN ANN RAIN 1731. WT WS RECAST 1932 MEARS AND STAINBANK, WHITECHAPEL FOUNDRY, LONDON [12th year of Queen Ann was in fact 1713 so even bellcasters can make typographical errors!]

The clock bell is inscribed JAMES SHELLY REDLINCH 1828

CYRIL CHURCHILL - 70 YEARS A BELLRINGER

One man stands out among bellringers in Downton. For over 70 of his 87 years Cyril Churchill was a bellringer. Born and bred in Downton he was Captain of the Bellringers and Keeper of the Tower for most of his adult life. He wound the church clock every day for 55 years. To do this he had to climb 50 steps, summer and winter. When the clock was eventually electrified in 1991 he was more than happy to be made redundant - but he kept on ringing until shortly before he died in March 1992.

A large congregation for his funeral heard the bells rung half-muffled both before and after the service. On 11 April, on 'his' bells, a peal of 5056 Cambridge Major [an intricate changing of the order in which bells are rung] was rung in thanksgiving for his life.

Cyril would have enjoyed many annual choir and bellringers' outings of which one envious choirboy remembered: *'The bellringers had a barrel of beer in the back of the coach and the Vicar his flask of gin in the front.'*

BELLRINGERS IN TROUBLE

Probably Cyril also knew that on 12 July 1845 the Salisbury and Winchester Journal reported that the reason the bells of St Laurence were not being rung was that the bellringers had, according to the Vicar, Rev. Richard Payne, been *'very properly dismissed by the Churchwardens for misconduct.'* Perhaps the barrel of beer in the back of the coach had been known to reach the bell chamber.....

Payne added that *'misrepresentations had been made in some London papers..... to which he did not think that any reply was necessary.'* The Journal gave Downton helpful advice on how to recruit a new set of ringers so that *'the melodious voices of the Downton bells may, as heretofore, joyfully herald in our great public festivals, and no occasion henceforth be given to cast even the shadow of a doubt upon the heartfelt loyalty of our good friends in Downton.'* At this distance and without research it may be guessed that Downton had failed to ring its bells to celebrate the birthday of Queen Victoria on 24 May.

RINGING FOR SPECIAL OCCASIONS

The bells are always rung for special occasions, local and national. A board in the ringing chamber records ringing for the Jubilee of King George V - May 6 1935 and the Coronation of King George VI - 12 May 1937. They were rung half muffled to honour the memory of King George VI on 6th February 1952. They were rung in full to commemorate the Coronation of Her Majesty, Queen Elizabeth II - 2nd June 1953.

Royal weddings and births, the end of the Gulf War with the Liberation of Kuwait and the freeing of the hostage Terry Waite after 1763 days in captivity in Lebanon have all been occasions for Downton peals to ring out.

RECTORS, VICARS AND PASTORS

On the whole Downton has been very fortunate in its clergy and many of them served around fifty years in office so they must have liked the village. While still a Rectory it was wealthy and many distinguished men held the office of Rector of Downton. They included one Cardinal, John de Columpna, of St. Angelo, who was one of several non-resident aliens holding income-bearing posts in the English church in the 13th and 14th Centuries.

In the Cardinal's case it seems to have been a way of paying him off for loans made during the Hundred Years War for, in 1346 the King, Edward III, took back *all fruits, provends and emoluments of the Church of Downton* - he was winning the war so could snub the Cardinal! Another absentee Rector went on to be Bishop of Hereford and custos of Ireland.

Early . . .

As we saw earlier, Bishop Wykeham of Winchester made Downton a Vicarage in 1383. Early vicars of Downton complained that the income without the Rector's Great Tithes was too little to cover their costs. They had to provide a number of curates to cover a very large Parish.

Winchester College gradually conceded more income to their Vicars and by the 18th Century Downton was relatively well endowed - well enough to attract a number of notable incumbents. Curiously, the little chapel at Standlynch remained a constant bone of contention with the Lord of Standlynch demanding that the Vicar of Downton give him a proper service, if you will forgive the pun.

. . . middle . . .

COMMUNICANT NUMBERS VARY LITTLE

The congregation taking Communion varied in the 18th and 19th Centuries between 120 and 150 - rather less than today. At first sight this seems to contradict the reports that communicants were so many that the Sacrament was administered not only at the four great festivals of the Church but also at the two Sundays following them. It could be relevant that while church attendance was obligatory confirmation was not.

. . . late style Capitals

Holy Communion was a relatively infrequent form of service at least from the Commonwealth until the last thirty or forty years of the 20th Century. This may surprise modern Church of England members used to the Eucharist almost every Sunday. For many centuries Communion was regarded with suspicion, smacking of the Catholic Mass and all sorts of doctrinal horrors, and was a Sacrament to be taken very seriously on the few occasions each year when it was given and taken.

We have looked earlier at William Wilkes, installed in Elizabeth's time and still in office in 1637. In the

Interregnum between Charles I and Charles II, Samuel Cox was Vicar. He was an active preacher and evidently in sympathy with some of the Commonwealth's Presbyterian ideas because he signed up to the Concurrent Testimony of 1648. Probably too much in sympathy as we find a new Vicar, a year after the Restoration, called William Gale.

Gale lasted from 1661 to 1715, 54 years, although he did not always live in Downton. Eight years before he retired the parishioners petitioned Winchester College to name one of the curates, George Gifford, to replace him when the time came for Gale to retire. This was because Gifford was so popular (and, doubtless, doing all the work already). In 1715 the College duly presented him to the Parish.

Nicholas Webb was Vicar from 1721 to 1775, as long as William Wilkes had been in office. He also held prebends [drew salaries from] Lincoln, St Paul's and Salisbury cathedrals. Thomas Lear followed him but at first he lived away and the parish was served again by a curate. Lear resigned the living at one point but was reappointed in 1799 and died in Downton in 1828. Of Lear it was written, admittedly on his memorial plaque, *'A more worthy, pious and excellent parish priest.... it would be difficult to describe.'* He looked after *'poor and ignorant'* parishioners and was not discouraged by *'profligacy, inattention and ingratitude.'* Clearly a man of his time.

Lear did a lot of building work to his Vicarage and the present appearance of Chalkhill House is largely due to him. (Chalkhill was an earlier Vicar who built the new vicarage.) Lear was married to Ethelinda *Shuckburgh* Hewett. That suggests that his interest in coming to Downton may have come from his wife's family connection with Downton and Moot House. It is as yet unexplained who the Rev Charles Shuckburgh was but he appears on many lists of the 'Great and Good' of Downton, usually after Rev Thomas Lear.

Liscombe Clarke succeeded Lear and from 1827 to 1836 was Archdeacon of Salisbury as well, employing two curates to look after Downton. It was he who had had built a 'spacious school room' near the church in 1834 and his widow left money for the school.

Chapter 12

Road and Rail and River

RAILWAY AND TURNPIKE

Part of the result of inclosure was that responsibilities for roads changed. The main Salisbury-Fordingbridge road was never turnpiked (turned into a toll road) but the road from Downton through Redlynch to Cadnam was, in 1832, ten years after the major awards of inclosures in the area. This makes sense as relatively few people lived along it and inclosure removed communal responsibility for many of the roads and lanes. Good roads were needed to link up with the ever-expanding rail network that then came no closer to Downton than Alderbury Junction.

The London and South Western Railway and some landowners opposed the Salisbury area farmers and tradesmen who wanted a branch line to avoid a long detour through Southampton when travelling to Wimborne, Poole and South Devon. The Salisbury and Dorset Junction Railway were not successful in getting an Act passed until 1861. This authorised the building of a single line 19 miles long from Alderbury Junction to West Moors. This saved 20-25 miles on the journey from Poole to Salisbury.

The construction began three years later on 3 February 1864 when *"a cheery crowd saw Countess Nelson from*

The new line bridged Lode Hill

147

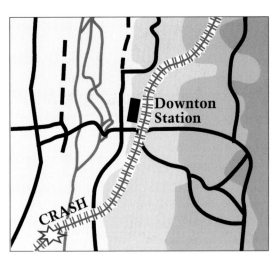

nearby *Trafalgar House at Downton, cut the first sod"*. And she also opened Downton Station on the arrival of the first train on 20 December 1866. It is said that the *bells of Salisbury Cathedral pealed joyfully* but L&SWR continued to make life difficult even although they were running the trains on it and taking 45% of the receipts. Their obstructive ways paid off, for them, and in 1883 they were able to buy the line cheaply.

DOWNTON'S RAILWAY DISASTER

On 3rd June 1884 the 4.50 train from Downton to Fordingbridge was one mile south of the station *'being driven like Jehu'** On an S-bend, with Pile Bridge at its centre, the middle coach was derailed just beyond the bridge. Seven carriages or vans ended in the meadow and two in a ditch with four feet of water. The three carriages in the centre were completely smashed. Five people were killed, two by drowning. Forty more were injured, several of them seriously. Professor Wright, his son and forty students at the nearby Downton Agricultural College came to rescue the passengers. The Rev Bunbury was in the second carriage and his next sermon gave 'Thanks' to God for his deliverance. Queen Victoria wrote sending her condolences. This was the worst train disaster up till this time.

The accident drew attention to the unregenerate attitude of the L&SWR towards rolling stock and track maintenance on its branch lines. The daughter of the Vicar of Downton, Constance Hill, reported that many of the *keys* had fallen out of the *chairs*, freeing the rails they were supposed to hold.

The crash was, indeed, attributed to the poor state of the track. This was, no doubt, L&SWR's way of saying it was the fault of the previous company rather than their time-keeping demands on their drivers. To keep to schedule they were used to approaching hills as fast as possible in order to get up them with the under-powered locomotives allocated by a grudging company to a line they did not like. Colonel Rich, the Board of Trade inspector, blamed the L&SWR.

*Jehu's driving was his hall mark. A lookout recognised him *'driving like a madman'* as he came to carry out a coup against Jehoram, King of Israel and Ahaziah, King of Judah on the instructions of the prophet Elisha.

THE ILLUSTRATED LONDON NEWS.

REGISTERED AT THE GENERAL POST-OFFICE FOR TRANSMISSION ABROAD.

No. 2356.—VOL. LXXXIV.　　　SATURDAY, JUNE 14, 1884.　　　WITH TWO SUPPLEMENTS{ SIXPENCE. By Post, 6½d.

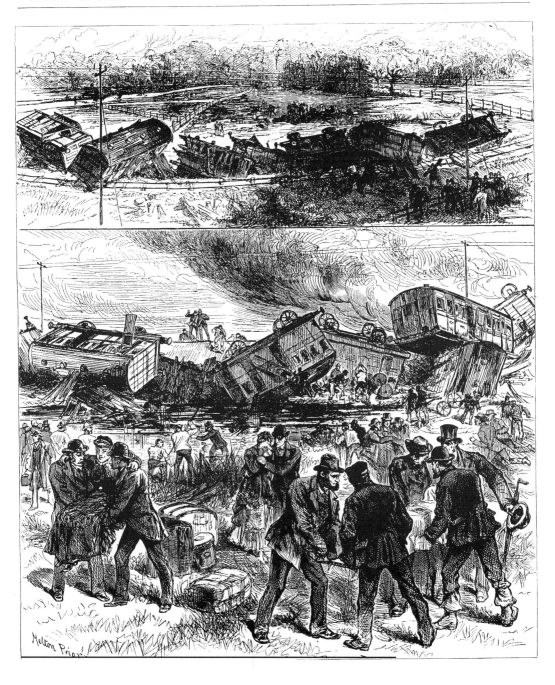

The Temple in the Moot

L&SWR continued to treat the line with disdain although it had a good excursion trade to Bournemouth and on several occasions brought in upwards of 3,000 people to enjoy festivals centred on the Moot to which people like Sybil Thorndike (later a Dame) came to perform. The winter timetable was as inconvenient as possible although the newspaper train down from London allowed late night revelry in Town. There were six trains each way every day.

The summer timetable in June 1901 was marginally better with 7 trains each way. It went through to Wimborne, Poole and Bournemouth taking an hour and forty minutes. The last 'up' train would carry anything up to 400 live eels taken from the Avon under the mills to be sold at Billingsgate early next morning.

WEEK-LONG EXCURSIONS

Paid holiday was a new idea - for a Council employee in 1936 one week a year was new and precious. He bought a ten shilling Runabout ticket for himself and for his son and each day for a week they would bicycle over the meadows from Gravel Close, across the waterfalls by Wild Weir, up in to Barford Park and then up past the Doctor's surgery to the station. The train would take them to a different place each day - Poole, Swanage, Lulworth - and then back at night, all on the one ticket.

KING GEORGE VI AND QUEEN ELIZABETH

There is one nice story from the later stages of World War II. Dr Whitehead, whose surgery was just below the station, was told by one of his patients that King George VI and Queen Elizabeth were coming to Downton by train. War time secrecy was very tight so how was it known so certainly? The Waiting Room floor was being scrubbed, apparently for the first time since it had been laid!

As so often, a countryman's wit and observation had outsmarted authority. Word got round and a sizeable crowd was there to greet Their Majesties who were visiting troops about to leave for France in 1940.

HIGH JINKS IN THE MOOT

Fetes and bazaars and concerts and plays and fireworks became a frequent feature of Downton at the turn of the 19th Century. Held in the Moot gardens by permission of their owner, E P Squarey, they were usually well attended with the railway running special excursions for visitors from as far afield as Poole, Wimborne and Salisbury. Some events lasted over three days. Most were for fund raising. The Public Hall, the Church and the village Nurse and Dispensary were all beneficiaries.

A regular feature was Mr Greet's company of Pastoral Players performing plays by Shakespeare. They came in 1898, 1902, and in 1908. In 1908 a Miss Sybil Thorndike in "The Comedy of Errors", was mentioned as playing Adriana *with a sympathetic sense of its strong dramatic qualities, the part suited her admirably and her characterisation was full of spirit.* Nice to hear that the redoubtable first Dame of English theatre was doing so well so young. She needed to as there had been heavy rain until mid-afternoon and even then *at times it was difficult to hear the speeches of the players, but this was due more to the sighing of the wind in the trees than to any defect in their playing.*

These events were organised by strong committees, sometimes of men, more usually of women. In 1898 Lady Goff of Hale House opened the Fete. Thereafter it seems more often to have been Countess Radnor who would start proceedings and there are remarks on how much the Earl has helped, *with his usual kindness.*

What stands out, as so often in Downton history, is how many Downton people were involved and giving of their talent. Choirs and bands and dancers; side show operators and stall holders; above all there were lots of children taking part even if their patriotic programme may seem a little dated today.

"You may call it a small bit of bunting,
You may say it's an old coloured rag,
But freedom has made it majestic,
And time has ennobled the flag"
they sang as they raised the Union Jack.

This followed Rule Britannia, Here's a Health unto His Majesty and One King, One Flag, One Fleet and, of course, God Save the King!

The King and Queen visited the wartime military headquarters at Breamore House - possibly the first monarch to do so since Queen Elizabeth and James I had each come to admire the new house. Princess Elizabeth, later Queen Elizabeth II, and Princess Margaret, as girls, were staying onboard the train and were seen by some.

DOWNTONIAN HONESTY

The Salisbury firm of Clark and Lush used Downton sidings as a coal depot for most of the 98 years that the line operated. Twenty varieties of coal and coke from South Wales and the Midlands were stored there. Clark and Lush applauded the villagers for their restraint - compared with the scale of coal thefts in Salisbury, Downtonians were honesty personified!

Sue Grice buys the last ticket

We hear little more of the Downton line until its closure on 4 May 1964 when 100 children from Downton took the last 'down' train, got off at Breamore and caught, almost at once because that was where 'up' and 'down' trains crossed, the 'up' train back to Downton. Government had brought in Dr Beeching, a former head of ICI, to try to make business sense of the woefully inefficient nationalised successor to the Southern Railway (which had taken over L&SWR), British Rail's Southern Region. He completed what L&SWR had long desired.

THE ROADS IMPROVE

From at least the 1720's there was a steady improvement to the Salisbury to Fordingbridge road which had been re-routed through the Headlands. It had originally gone past New Court, down Gravel Close, past the White Horse and on down South Lane probably ever since the Borough was built in 1209.

The Bull Inn served the passing trade on the new road as soon as a regular stagecoach service was started. 150 years later it felt some pressure as the railways gradually siphoned off the stagecoach passengers. Resourcefully, the Bull attracted a new kind of custom as it became possible for fisherman to come much more easily on the train from further afield. The 'Bull' of Bull Inn came to refer to the bull trout - the larger, male, trout - and the sign outside was of a handsome fish, not the leader of the herd. It was famous as a fishing inn till well after the Second World War.

Its sign today depicts a bull trout leaping in front of a bull!

ROAD MAINTENANCE

From 1555 each parish became responsible for its own roads and the inhabitants each had to give 6 days labour every year to their upkeep. Richer people had to provide a horse and cart as well. There was not a lot of wheeled traffic even at the end of the 17th Century but as trade increased so did the ruts. The Industrial Revolution might have been stillborn except that the government made the building and running of turnpike [toll] roads easy and attractive for private enterprise.

Eventually there were 1,100 turnpike trusts but parishes remained responsible for all the side roads and the 6 days Statute labour was inadequate. Very often the paupers on Poor Law relief were coerced into working on them. Towns were still cut off in winter and had to lay in salted stores to see them through. It was not until the Scottish road engineer Macadam began the use of tar or bitumen to bind the top surface that roads could cope with the huge increase in traffic. In Downton that did not begin until 1930 when, on the Salisbury-Fordingbridge road, to use the jargon of the time, *'the Trinidad came through'* - a huge bitumen lake in Trinidad was the main source of tar. Possibly the first Englishman to see that lake was Sir Walter Raleigh who noted it in his Commonplace book.

GARAGES

The other need for the new motor traffic was motor car maintenance. After the First World War, the returning soldiers had new skills. Mr Crisp had lived with his family in a tied house in Salisbury.

When he joined the Army in 1917, without being conscripted, his firm expelled his family from their home and they moved to Downton. On his demobilisation he set up Headlands Garage and stayed there until the Second World War.

During WW2 he was employed at Poole maintaining naval vessels and after the war he and his family stayed on. Others have run the same business ever since and the demand for garages and their number has steadily increased.

The Shell petrol station, next door and also on land previously owned by the Crisps, was sold to the England family in 1981.

They formed the Downton Motor Co and today they are Hyundai main dealers and Renault brokers.

BRIDGE REPAIRS NEEDED

In February 1898 the Parish Magazine had complained that Mill Bridge had been marked *'Unsafe'* for far too long:

Looking up High Street before the cottages (facing) were demolished to widen the road

'We have every right to complain that....such an all-powerful body as the County Council, to whom we entrust the care of our highways, should feel obliged to hesitate so long before doing anything.'

It goes on to explain that part of the trouble is the history of ownership *of* the bridge.

'When the Manor Mill was removed from the weirs above Catherine Mead and erected in Downton, the bridge over the mill stream would, of course, have been provided by those who gained advantage from the mill. .... when the bridge was last rebuilt, the Bishop of Winchester, as the then Lord of the Manor, contributed the timber from The Earldom's Woods, and others shared in the expense.'

WHY SHOULD THE FREEHOLDERS OF WICK PAY FOR THE BRIDGE?

This may date from before the Borough was created in 1209. In those days Downton was wholly east of the river. The best roads started from Downton whether to Salisbury, London or Southampton. Those who lived west of the river could well think it worth their while to build bridges and perhaps the Bishop required it of them once he had provided the timber.

Apparently the four eastern arches were the responsibility of the freeholders of Wick, the four centre arches belonged to the owners of the mills and the three western ones were attached to leasehold property then forming part of the paper mill.

Even in 1600 a map showed there was no proper road south to Fordingbridge from Wick although it may be inferred that there was a track south from the Borough Cross and the main road, starting with Gravel Close ran north past New Court to Charlton.

RIVER TRAFFIC

Early in Downton's history the river may have been an even more important thoroughfare than the few tracks and lanes. It continued to be used for trade until well into the 18th Century for horse-drawn barges. From time to time, proposals to canalise the Avon were brought up. Tunnel Hill near Alderbury is a reminder of the last, failed, attempt to do so. Some of the works came as far as Downton.

The London to Weymouth road still went through Downton in the 1730s

The story of Raleigh bringing a ship up to Downton to break it up and use the timbers in Parsonage Manor has never been verified. It is plausible. There is however a well documented voyage up the river by John Taylor, a London waterman. In August 1623 he and four others, two of them Salisbury men, had brought a wherry round the coast from London and up through Downton. A wherry was a substantial passenger boat, able to carry a sail, which was more suitable for estuary work than such a sea-going passage.

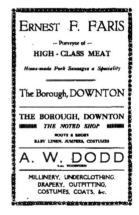

John Taylor made a number of such journeys which were often in the character of a sponsored walk - punters were invited to promise to buy his account of whatever adventure he was proposing. Towards the end of his Salisbury book he writes a long section appealing to its citizens to realise how much better off they would be if they opened up their river to trade.

'the dearness of the carriages eats up all your commodities and profit; which commodity may be avoided, if your river be cleansed: and what man can tell what good in time may redound to your city from the sea, by foreign goods, which may be brought in to Christchurch Haven by shipping?'

He seems to have been well received by Sir Edward Gorges at Longford Castle but not by the Herberts at Wilton. He badgered everyone with his ideas - *'my fruitless and worthy lip-labour, mix'd with a deal of airey and non-substantial matter.'* That there may have been a surfeit of words is suggested by one observer who said that after two or three enjoyable days in his company *'afterwards you were entertained with* **crambe bis cocta'** - yesterday's reheated cabbage!

CARS AND BUSES

The coming of the car and omnibus led to a steady improvement to roads, especially after the First World War. Tarmac was gradually used on all roads so that by 1939 it was unusual to find an 'adopted' road that had not been made up.

Connell's yellow bus and Buddens' Skylark (still running today) were among the first bus services and between the Wars there was a regular bus service from Salisbury. Excursions were as often by coach as by train. After the Second World War road traffic of all sorts doubled and redoubled. Within a century Downton had gone from quiet farming community with a few small industries manned almost entirely by villagers to a busy commuter settlement with most using car or bus to get to work away from Downton.

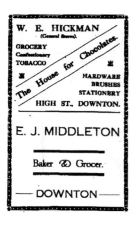

Chapter 13

War, Peace and Downton

FROM DOWNTON PARISH MAGAZINE AT THE TURN OF THE 19th CENTURY -

QUEEN VICTORIA'S 80TH BIRTHDAY

'On the 80th birthday of our Gracious Queen the loyalty of some of us could not be restrained and we paraded the village, waving our flags and singing ourselves hoarse to the strains of the National Anthem....we then retired to the vicarage lawn, made speeches, indulged in confections, and like true Britishers, wound up with "Hip, hip, hurrah". June 1899, Parish Magazine.

THE BOER WAR

Mr Squarey, the owner of the Moot was very much top village citizen of his time. Mrs Squarey's brother was General Tucker who had just been appointed to a command in South Africa. The Boer War was by this time a major public concern. It started at the end of 1899 and was not going well. Mafeking and Ladysmith were under siege. The Boer *commandos'* families had been pulled in from the outlying farms in to camps - concentration camps - so that they could no longer support their men in their guerrilla campaign. 26,000 died in those camps, mainly of disease and, in particular, measles. We from Britain lost 100,000 men.

Downton, with many young men away fighting, did little to mark the turn of the century on 1 January 1900.

A Downton couple, Mr and Mrs Noyce, and a Mrs Harrison each received a special Bounty of £2 [late 1990's value perhaps £200] sent personally by Queen Victoria because they had four sons each serving in the Army. This was at a time when the war was beginning to be won. Kimberley was relieved in February and Mafeking in June to widespread rejoicing.

BUT LIFE WENT ON...

The same issue of the Parish Magazine condemned the *'thoughtless and foolish practice of stone throwing and to the dangers to the public which it causes.'* *'A stone is very easily thrown by a lad e.g. at a train from a railway bridge but very serious injury may be caused by it'.* So vandalism is not new.

In October 1900 there was a General Election and the Magazine chose to comment: *'It is hardly necessary in these days to say that beyond all else at Election-times such things as needless disturbances of the peace or drunkenness are to be deprecated in every way. Such times as these are apt to cause such offences if people give way to temptations which, indeed, are always present, but are so especially during Election seasons.'* It would seem that Downton's old election traditions died hard.

Jones the Butcher shows off his prize-winning stock

DOWNTON'S MARTYR

Emily Whitchurch, one of the Whitchurch family who were great benefactors of the South Lane Baptist Church, went out to China in 1884 with the China Inland Mission. She was an active missionary and took great satisfaction from the destruction of idols.

It was alien intrusions like hers which led to a series of anti-foreigner uprisings culminating in the Boxer rebellion of 1899. In July 1900 Miss Whitchurch was martyred. She and her companion missionary were clubbed to death.

QUEEN VICTORIA DIES

In January 1901 Queen Victoria died, our oldest and longest reigning monarch. *'Even in this little village everyone tried to show their affection and reverence for the great Mother Queen, so suddenly taken from us.'* Most of the congregation were dressed in black and the church was draped for mourning. *'The lessons at Morning Service were read (as is usually the case) by the Earl Nelson, the only surviving Peer who held his title when Her Majesty came to the throne.'*

THE 3RD EARL NELSON

The third Earl Nelson was a great character. He was a regular attender in the House of Lords and was also much involved locally in Downton. He married Mary Jane Diana Agar, a daughter of Lord Normanton of Somerley.

Later in life Lady Mary became a Roman Catholic and it would seem her sons followed her but her husband definitely didn't and remained an active Church of England member until his death in 1913. After the third Earl's death that Standlynch chapel below the big house was *'blessed, restored to Catholic worship and rededicated to Mary, Queen of Angels, St Michael and All the Angels'* on June 20th 1914.

The third Earl was evidently keen to show his interest in the village and its domestic arrangements. On one occasion he quizzed one of his fellow parishioners : *"How long do you wear your shirt, my man?"*

A puzzled pause was followed by: *"Three inches below mi'arse, Milord."* Deference to the last.

NO CORONATION BUT CELEBRATIONS
JUST THE SAME

King Edward and Queen Alexandra who followed the old Queen were to have been crowned on 26 June 1902 and Downton made great preparations. The first Coronation in 65 years in 1902 was another excuse for a party in Downton. Lord Nelson allowed the use of Barford Park for a day-long programme of celebrations on 27 June. The preparations for it were almost complete when the King had appendicitis. He survived and it didn't take the village long to decide to have the party even if there was no Coronation!

The procession formed at the Borough Cross with nine organisations taking part and two bands. The streets were only partially decorated as much had not been completed before hearing of the King's illness.

From 2 o'clock there were Old Fashioned Athletic Sports which had items like the Egg and Spoon Race and Climbing the Greasy Pole. Just to keep the jollity at its peak there was also a Ladies, 100 yards, Flat Race - the men were restricted to Throwing

Coronation picnic in Barford Park

the Cricket Ball and, no doubt, the Three-Legged Race.

> 4 p.m. to 6 p.m. — Tea, consisting of Beef, Mutton, Ham, Cake, Bread, Butter, Tea etc;
> 6 p.m. — Comic Football Match "Clowns versus Niggers" (arranged by Downton Boys' Football Club.)
> 7 p.m. till 9.15 p.m. — Dancing
> It was decided not to go through with the final part of the programme which would have been:
> 9.15 p.m. — Torchlight Procession to Barford Down
> 10.00 p.m. — Bonfire on Barford Down
> Finale: "GOD SAVE THE KING".

However on 30 June the King was so recovered that the torchlight procession and bonfire were hastily put together again and went ahead. 40 stood round in a circle with their torches aloft, singing God Save the King and other patriotic airs.

On 9 August the King was well enough to be crowned and so there were further celebrations, this time in the Moot. The procession had Decorated Cars and went down to the Headlands before turning round to go to the Moot. Each child was given a Coronation bun and then there was a concert. Fireworks did not go well - damp squibs? - but torch bearers and Maypole dancers did various manoeuvres round the fish pond and no one was going to let the evening go sour. The evening ended by processing back through the village to the Square [by the King's Arms and Chemist] singing and having a happy time.

FIRST WORLD WAR 1914 - 1918

For those who want to understand the cost of the First World War, which ended a period of twelve years of peace under King Edward and then King George V, a visit to the Memorial Hall is a salutary reminder of human folly and frailty. Look not only at the twenty-four names of those who died, displayed outside, but also at the Memorial Board inside listing those 240 young men from a village of 1,750 - virtually every able bodied man - who left family and job to fight in the War to End All Wars.

Their four long years in the mud and horror of Flanders or at sea in the first war in which death from torpedo or mine was a constant threat is a terrible condemnation of national leaderships without vision. One in ten did not come home.

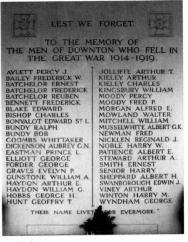

The 44 who died in the wider parish of Downton

WAR AND PEACE - FATE STEPS IN

Most who survived the horror of Flanders mud never forgot and seldom spoke.

Frank Bundy, however, had a strange tale to tell. He was lying, severely wounded, in No Man's Land between the German and British trenches in France, when a German army patrol came upon him. He thought he had bought it and didn't much care. To his amazement the German Sergeant began speaking to him in English. *"Is that the Wiltshire Regiment you belong to?"* he said, pointing at the badge on Bundy's shoulder. *"Do you happen to know a village called Downton near Salisbury?"* Frank couldn't believe his ears and even less so when the Sergeant suddenly exclaimed: *"Gott in Himmel. Frank...is that you?"*

The Sergeant was none other than the pre-war butler from Trafalgar House whom Frank knew well. Astonishingly, he was the only German Frank Bundy had ever met.

Frank was rescued, survived and lived to old age back in Downton. In later years he was gardener to Dr Whitehead at Hamilton House and delighted the doctor's grandchildren with his Soldiers' French.

The widows and orphans of those killed were not well looked after by the State. The British Legion, started then

to look after them and the thousands of disabled and shell-shocked survivors, has continued its valiant work ever since.

It was little compensation to those widows that, in grudging acknowledgment of their wartime efforts, women - over 30 years old - were given the vote in 1918.

One war-damaged soldier was returned to Downton and his family. From time to time his condition worsened and he would be unable to work for months at a time. A grateful nation did nothing for him. He belonged to the 'Downers Club' which was a mutual society for village workers to cover sickness and unemployment [Possibly the local nickname for the 1788 Downton Society which survived in to the 1920's?]. This paid out four shillings per week when he was unable to work. Fortunately the British Legion paid a further ten shillings a week or else, as his son put it, *'We would have died of starvation.'*

It is hard to provide a valid comparison with today but when the Government of the day imposed a one shilling a day reduction in pay for all ranks of the armed forces they apparently did not realise the consequences for the lowest ranks who were only getting four shillings a day at the outset.

KING GEORGE REVIEWS HIS FLEET

Many from Downton took the train excursions to Portsmouth, forty miles to the east, to see the Review of the Fleet. The Solent was crammed with hundreds of warships anchored in line after line. On the day, the King steamed by their serried ranks in his Royal Yacht "Victoria and Albert."

The ships were dressed overall with bunting stretched from stem to stern. Sailors lined the side, cheering their monarch. In the evening there was a searchlight display, fireworks and then, at a signal, every ship switched on rows of lights which outlined their hulls.

In Downton those that listened to their wireless sets for the live description by the BBC heard Tommy Woodroffe, the commentator and a former naval officer, rather over-entertained by his former shipmates, say the immortal words: *'The Fleetsh all lit up... we're all lit up'* to be followed by silence as the BBC pulled the plug. Poor Tommy. A good party.

DISILLUSION AND DEPRESSION

All too quickly people realised that the War had cured nothing. There were difficult times not helped by inept government attitudes.

Poor economic conditions persisted. Unemployment insurance and pay started, Old Age Pensions were introduced, agricultural wages were subject to decision by local Boards but some farmers responded by sacking workers. It was not a happy time. Then came the 1930 Stock Market crash followed by years of economic depression and high unemployment.

Hitler and Mussolini threatened and it was with some relief that the nation celebrated the Silver Jubilee of King George V and Queen Mary. In Downton there were street parties and a procession with floats. Flags and bunting decorated houses and streets. The bells were rung. Whether the newly converted mills had actually started generating hydroelectric power in time for illuminations is not clear but they were to supply Downton with electricity from that year until their closure in 1972. Sadly, the old King was dying of smoking-induced lung cancer so Downton was soon to mourn. Within a year there followed the unsettling abdication of the new King Edward VIII and ever nastier news from Germany and still far too high unemployment.

Believed to be Royal Horse Artillery on the Borough in the '20s

There was another happy time with the Coronation in 1937 of King George VI and his beloved Queen Elizabeth. This was followed by another Review of the Fleet, not quite such a large gathering as in 1935 and, ominously, with a very impressive brand-new German pocket-battleship representing the military threat of Hitler and his Nazis.

Chamberlain, Munich, the invasion of Poland, evacuation of children from the great towns and another war followed one another with bewildering speed.

SECOND WORLD WAR 1939 - 1945

Future generations may find it hard to imagine how the first war to bring ordinary people in to the front line felt to

1939 ——— 1945
RICHARD CRISP
CECIL J. GRACE
CECIL J. F. MORGAN
CECIL H. W. PHILLIPS
HENRY E. PHILLIPS
ARTHUR S. PRIDDICE
WILLIAM F. G. REYNOLDS
PERCY D. RIDOUT
VIOLET SHELLY
WILLIAM C. STICKLEY

Dunkirk survivors get their first taste of England . . .

those ordinary people. Downton had been supplying regular soldiers and sailors and, more recently, airmen for many generations. For the depressed agricultural areas of the south, the armed forces were a logical outlet for young men who had grown up with country values of service, duty and patriotism.

To start with it was another case of 'It'll all be over by Christmas.' Then came the cruel reality of Blitzkrieg and Dunkirk in 1940 and a frantic throwing up of defences against Hitler's imminent invasion. The River Avon was one of a series of lines of defence against what was expected to be the German plan of attack.

Bridges were mined, blockhouses were built and the area was garrisoned with troops. One of those men was an artillery man stationed in Downton in August 1940. He was part of 5 Corps commanded by a little known Major-General called Montgomery.

BLOCKHOUSES

Few of the wartime defences remain but an interesting example can be seen at the Mill on the Woodgreen-Breamore road, on the River Avon south of Downton. Gun embrasures in one of the buildings show how a wide angle could be covered. By using an existing building some camouflage was given. There were many blockhouses round Downton but almost all were removed.

Women and boys gather the wartime harvest

The gunner was billeted with a retired Judge and his wife, opposite The Bull. Many were billeted in other local houses. One 70-year old man had six soldiers in his home.

The artillery man remembers the Dad's Army quality of their tactical thinking. They cut branches and laid them beside the Fordingbridge Road. When German tanks were expected the branches would be dragged across the road, the tanks would stop to clear the road and while the hatch was open a brave Englishman would lob a hand-grenade in to the tank.

Dad's Army itself, the Local Defence Volunteers (LDV) who were to be renamed the Home Guard, took on most of the patrolling and guarding duties.

THE BOROUGH CROSS

The Cross set in the middle of Downton Borough is very ancient, perhaps dating back to 1210. Little of the original now exists except, probably, the cross at the very top.

It has been destroyed or badly damaged at least twice - in 1642 on orders from Cromwell's Parliament, and in 1940 when a German landmine landed in New Court meadows. A sketch in the 18th century shows only a windvane or similar and the cross damaged in the war was a 19th Century addition.

We know that the present top found close by in 1952, is many hundreds of years old. In the words of an expert stonemason it had been *"cut across the Lace"* (the grain of the stone) which has not been done for hundreds of years.

Lord Radnor gave the Chilmark stone needed to replace the broken shaft. The cross now looks the same as one of the few mediaeval town crosses which survived the Parliamentary troops' destruction.

An anti-aircraft battery was sited on Barford Down towards Pepperbox Hill. Some of its men were billeted in the 'Wooden Spoon' and use was made of the golf course which had been built on the Downs.

13C.?

LAND MINE ON THE WATERMEADOWS

A landmine, or possibly two, fell in the water meadows between the church and New Court.

18C.

The explosion shattered glass and blew out doors over a large area and damaged the church. It toppled the Borough Cross which was not properly repaired until 1952.

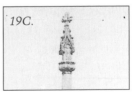

19C.

An aircraft crash landed up Barford Lane. A small boy rushed up to see whether he could help but the aircraft caught fire. He could do nothing and the pilot was unable to get out. Many went to see a German Junkers 88 bomber that crashed a few miles south-east of Downton in the New Forest. A stick of bombs was jettisoned on Wick Down and another bomb blast blocked Slab Lane making life difficult for returning revellers.

Today . . .

To distract night attacks from the cities there was a dummy 'city' built on the western face of Clearbury Down,

LIFE IN WARTIME

Someone writing from the area in 1944, not long before the invasion of Normandy, may catch a little of the flavour of wartime Downton. Her letters were written to cousins in Canada to keep in touch and thank them for food and clothing sent to ease the pain of rationing. Her husband was away at sea in the Royal Navy.

'I am writing this in bed to save doing the blackout downstairs and it is now very late because I was interrupted by an Air Raid Warning and some gunfire. I don't usually bother to look out these days, but tonight I felt I must, just to see from which direction the gunfire was coming - and so I got a magnificent front seat view of the end of an enemy.

There he was, the little silver victim, at the apex of a great triangle of light and round him the dull red flashes of the bursting shells. The searchlights were concentrated on him from all directions and his attempts to escape seemed pathetically futile - and yet the shells seemed to be bursting far short of him. But he staggered - dropped and rose again and seemed to hesitate. I was not conscious of the sound of his engines and even the gun fire was vague and distant across the valley but in the garden the nightingale tried a few exploratory notes.

The silver enemy became a globe of flame - way behind it a small white speck sank slowly earthwards held in the light of two or three searchlights. The others shut off with a suddenness that hurt but they were no longer needed as the globe of flame became a streak of earthbound light. It rushed behind the hill and a great blaze lighted the sky. Minutes afterwards, it seemed, I heard the scream of a diving aircraft and a shattering explosion. But the nightingale was undisturbed and was by now in very good voice.'

She goes on later

'Night and day the roar of planes is almost continuous. The Battle of Britain and the subsequent bombing of Plymouth and Liverpool which we experienced, horrible though they were, were a mere shadow of what is now being handed out to the Germans. .....when I consider that the planes we hear going out are probably only a small portion of the attack and I think back to compare the volume of sound with what I remember from the days when we were the target I pity the Germans.'

On 20th May 1944, a fortnight before the invasion, she resumes the letter

'I suppose you are just as tensely waiting for the first news of the new invasion as we are [It was to be on 6th June] ... some evenings when the air attack has been heavy all day and the lull between waves of aircraft is filled with the sound of heavy traffic I think "They are starting now".... since before Easter we have been in a restricted area and people outside it cannot come in to see us. We are often asked for our identity cards and illegitimate travellers are quite ruthlessly sent back.'

In a later letter in July, after the invasion, she talks of the problem of kitting out a son for school.

'It will require 75 coupons and our normal allowance is 24 for five months, I think! Children get 10 extra, normally, and large children get an extra 20 so he should have 50 altogether and I shall go naked! Boys shoes take 7 coupons and, if he has to take man's sizes, 9 coupons.'

She describes a journey to London and the problems of overcrowding and delays. It was at the time that flying bombs had started.

'One of the "Doodle-bugs"[V1 flying bombs] flew over sounding like a flying tank - the engine went suddenly silent and then came the explosion just as the newspapers had described it. What interested me was the calmness of the lunchers whose lives undoubtedly were in very great danger. It actually fell about a mile away so we felt nothing.'

She had talked to a London friend who helped in the rescue work and said they had had 10 "incidents" [Some of them probably V2s, the first ballistic missiles] in 5 days but was constantly amazed by the quiet courage of the women in her Women's Volunteer Service and the skill of the National Fire Service and Heavy Rescue people.

On the way home: 'We waved to many train loads of troops at the big stations and passed several huge hospital trains - American mostly - but fortunately empty.'

This was truly a war that touched all.

Wartime wooden military telephone wire insulators

1943-44 US Army Camp
('Windmill Camp' or 'Tintown')

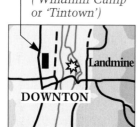

to the north west of the village, with two RAF men waiting there to ignite it so that German bombers would be fooled into bombing open fields instead of their real target.

THE AMERICANS

Downton was in the heart of the preparation area for D Day and there was a large American camp where the Industrial Estate is now built. It was known as Windmill Camp after the wind pump in its midst. Later it was known as Tin Town after the corrugated-iron roofs, shaped in a half circle, of the Nissen huts in which they lived.

The lorries and jeeps and tanks being gathered for the invasion of Normandy were dispersed over every available bit of wasteland, scrub and moorland.

The place was alive with jeeps and G.I.s. They found England quaint and primitive and cute. The lad who delivered the milk used the time-honoured system of generations: a medium sized churn was taken round to customers and the milk served into jugs with a measure. The Yanks were soon demanding to try this milk and the boy carried a glass to serve them for perhaps a rather higher price than he could charge the villagers.

The girls have especial memories of that time. HiFi Henry used to set up dances several nights a week in the Memorial Hall. He achieved miracles with old 78 rpm bakelite dance band records. A great time was had by all. What went on in the Memorial Gardens next door when the music ended was highly educational to the young and innocent.

Longford Castle

The headquarters were at Longford Castle and officers and men soon discovered that the River Avon had good fishing. Very unorthodox methods were used and fish stocks rapidly fell. Fortunately, and perhaps with a little seductive encouragement from the Castle, the US General developed a passion for fishing. Very soon the fishing was highly organised and controlled with military police serving as under-keepers. Such under-keepers: they patrolled with their carbines cocked!

Chapter 14

Downton ready for its next Millennium

TRADES AND INDUSTRIES IN THE 2OTH CENTURY

Downton suffered in the years that followed both wars. Farming was still depressed with cheap imports from Australia, New Zealand and Canada and too little new employment came to the village.

There was a tanner in Downton in 1215. Edmund Snelgrove may have been in Downton tanning from the 1560's with his sons succeeding him as tanners. Tanning was a significant industry through the 18th and 19th Centuries supporting shoe, glove and harness makers. John Gibbs, father and son, George Hooper and, in 1903, Nobes and Hunt, were all tanners. Then in 1919 the Southern Tanning Company was formed and they built the large tannery building we now see.

The old Tannery

Around 1930, in the Great Depression, that company failed and was succeeded by the Downton Tanning Company Ltd who, under new ownership, survived and at times even prospered until 1998. They produced high quality leather mainly for saddles and harness. As the millennium ends the Tannery is in the hands of developers hoping to find a mix of housing to build there which will be acceptable to the Planners and the village.

Paper was made at the Downton mill at least from 1714 to 1914 and specialised in hand-made writing-paper.

BOOKER'S BEGINNINGS IN DOWNTON

Bacon curing was already in Downton by 1923. In 1929 the old Workhouse, built in 1730, was converted into a smokehouse. Production increased to 100 pig carcases a week. I. Beer took it over in 1934 and increased production to 500 pigs a week.

Yet again, this time as part of Fitch Lovell, the factory was enlarged and by 1956 the staff of around 100 were handling 1,600 pigs a week. Until that factory closed in 1968 it was producing bacon, sausages, hams and cooked meats.

The company then moved to new warehouses in Salisbury Road where I.Beer had already moved its retail distribution arm. There were many changes of ownership and strategy in the following years.

Today the Downton depot employs around 150 people, many of them local, and turns over approximately £38 million per annum. It distributes a wide variety of catering products to around 750 customers a day. Their laden lorries leave early in the morning to disperse across the south.

Booker Foodservices is now one element of a global conglomerate with South African ownership. There are plans for expansion in Downton.

BREWING COMES BACK TO DOWNTON

Many if not most of the large number of inns, alehouses, tipplers and other purveyors of alcoholic drink in Downton brewed their own beer.

In 1992, in that long tradition of brewing enterprise, Hopback Brewery chose Downton. They saw it as a good place for distribution to its many wholesale and Free House customers and to the six pubs it owns. It has room here for expansion and Downton has good water.

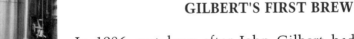

Having acquired The Bull, Hopback has undertaken a thorough and long-overdue refurbishment of that fine old coaching inn.

GILBERT'S FIRST BREW

In 1986, not long after John Gilbert had taken over the Wyndham Arms in Salisbury, he started making beer there. His first beer, called G.F.B. (Gilbert's First Brew!) sold well, won several awards.

Now there are five Hopback brands which have won over 60 awards. A very small staff - 3 brewers and 12 others - are hectically busy but have managed to keep a family atmosphere. As the century ends they are committing themselves to stay and expand in Downton.

> **Hopback: A brewer's vessel with a false perforated bottom which receives from the copper the unfermented infusion of malt and hops and strains out the hops. A sort of sieve! Hopback Brewery use modern equipment and don't actually have one.....!**

Mitchell's Timber and Builders' Merchants had their depot on Lode Hill and the brickmaking kilns along Moot Lane. Today the depot is Tucker Engineering and the brickworks have re-opened with new owners. The local clay makes handsome red bricks but they are extremely porous.

Downton Engineering at Mesh Pond started in 1934 as a motor garage. During the war it made brass shell cases and fuses. After the war, under Daniel Richmond and his brother, tuned high performance cars and became world famous for its 'Cooper' version of the Mini. Mini-Coopers are much prized even today.

MODERN LIGHT INDUSTRY

On the Industrial Estate there are a number of technically advanced small industries with the biggest, ColourCare International, the film processing firm, having grown from the photographic processing operation started in a small Salisbury shop by Stanley Adams after the Second World War.

It has changed hands and grown many times since and is currently owned by its Directors. It is international and the largest independent photo processing company in the UK. Downton Laboratory is the largest in the group and in the UK.

It processes over 5,000,000 films a year, almost all overnight. 100 vans cover the south of England, driving over 5,000,000 miles a year. During the summer months ColourCare employs over 400 people. Even in winter there are 300.

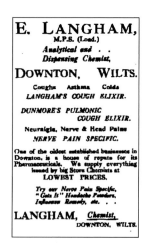

Intex Vending supply and maintain high quality drink and snack vending machines - a far cry from the penny-in-the-slot machines which graced Downton station a century before. They employ 22 people and have turnover of £1.2 million.

Phillips Produce are specialised food distributors, mainly to restaurants and delicatessens. They have 35 people working with them.

Southern Counties Watersoftener Services meet the needs of a hard water area supplying, fitting and maintaining a wide range of industrial and domestic treatment plants......and so the story goes on.

Downton's industry is small, high quality and forward looking, and so perhaps a reflection of the village itself.

DUNMORE, MAN OF MANY PARTS

ColourCare has a fascinating antecedent in Downton. From 1850 to 1900 Mr Dunmore was the village chemist. He was known to go up to London every Friday by train and there were dark rumours about who he might be seeing there..... In fact he was one of the very first professional photographers and his studio was in London. A further kink to the story is that he also exported his Sunset Dip to sheep farmers all over the world and today in Downton BBW Cropcare exports agro-chemicals to farmers world-wide.

Dunmore knew his market and produced Dunmore's Pulmonic Cough Elixir. Langham, his successor, continued to sell it, no doubt to satisfy local demand, but he also offered Langham's Cough Elixir which dealt with a subtly different set of symptoms.

Their successor, as the 20th Century ends, Jane Baldrey, not only has her own special cough medicine, Mr Linesley's Famous Derbyshire Cough Mixture, but has plans to provide remedial massage, foot care and a beauty therapist! An enterprising profession.

CHAMBERLIN'S VEGETABLE COUGH PILLS,
For Coughs, Colds, Hoarseness, Shortnesss of Breath, &c., &c.

These Pills the Proprietor can with the greatest confidence recommend for the above complaints; they will allay irritation in the chest and throat, which excite coughing, promote expectoration, and remove phlegm.—*Sold in boxes at* 7½d., 1s. 1½d., *and* 2s. 9d. *each.*

... and a rival!

TROUT FISHERY

Trafalgar Fisheries started farming trout in Barford Park in the mid-70's. Today the site covers 50 acres of former water meadows. The farm needs a continuous supply of fresh water through its ponds and this is taken from the old carriers.

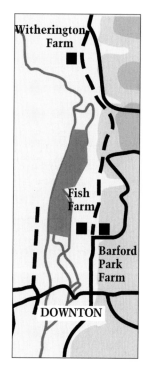

The main species grown is the Rainbow Trout but Brown and Golden Trout and American Brook Charr are also farmed. On a smaller scale, ornamental fish, Koi Carp and Golden Orfe are produced.

Trafalgar Fisheries employ thirty-one people at the Barford site and produce about 900 tons of trout per year. This makes it the largest trout farm in the country.

MEDICAL CARE

The earliest reference to a doctor practising in Downton comes from the Workhouse records. In 1784 Mr Sheffield, surgeon, is paid £10.0s.0d for six months work. The rent for six months was £11.0s.0d and the subscription to Salisbury Infirmary was £5.5s.0d while the man who looked after the Borough received £23.....values change.

When Sheffield died in 1798 the Salisbury Journal noted his passing. Apparently he was well respected but eccentric. This was borne out by his instruction in his Will that he was to be buried in his garden on Waterside and that when his favourite horse died it was to be buried with him.

He was no doubt somewhat vexed, wherever he was, when he was exhumed and reburied with his wife in 1807. However in this century it is said that the bones of a horse were found in a garden in Waterside so that, at least, he accomplished.

Quacks were still a problem in Victoria's time - 'Punch' had a suggestion

Early in the 19th Century a medical charity was operating in Downton. It seems to have been funded mainly by the rich although some form of regular saving by potential patients ensured them priority treatment. It seems likely that the Workhouse sickbay was not thought adequate and for a time the large house on the corner of Slab Lane was a fever hospital. It still shows the later signs for Reffell's Butcher's shop.

In 1868 or 69 the Downton Cottage Hospital was established. Admission was free for 'persons resident in the Parish' eligible for Parochial relief. Others living in Downton could be admitted to the Hospital 'on payment varying from 3s.6d. to 7s. per week, according to their means, and with consent of the Doctor.' They were required to bring clean linen with them and replace it 'once a-week, or oftener if necessary.'

First one and then two nurses were employed. Latterly they were housed in the house now on the corner of Moot Lane. This could, apparently, accommodate some patients but it seems unlikely that it was the original Hospital.

The old nurses' house

In the year of 1872, 17 cases were treated in the Cottage Hospital. Inflammation of the lungs, bronchitis, rheumatic fever, dropsy, carbuncle, consumption and Bright's disease are listed ailments. Nine were discharged cured, six died in Hospital and two remained under treatment. The report commented that the reason the deaths were so high was because it had been an unusually healthy year and so some cases of consumption were afforded 'the comforts and nursing at the last moments, which they could not have in their own homes, rather than with any hope of cure.' An early hospice.

The average cost of each patient was about 14 shillings. The nurse's wages for the year were £20.16s. Patients who had to pay contributed £3.13s.6d. - approximately 10 bed/weeks - but the main income was from subscriptions by the wealthy of the village.

Probably the old hospital

There is a reference to a Dr Hamming, in the 1850s, and to E.A. Kemp-Welch MD, in 1863, living in the village. Hamming was on the Downton Dispensing Committee. It is not until the 1890's that Dr Whiteley is known for sure to be the village Doctor.

He was another eccentric - and irascible with it. He always wore a top hat and went round his practice in a pony and trap. As soon as cars were available locally, he bought one. That was in 1906 and it was one of the first three built in Salisbury.

He (or, perhaps his successor, Dr Whitehead) built a 9 hole golf course on Barford Down which seems to have survived in to the Second World War - but not after it

THE WHITEHEAD ERA

Whiteley was succeeded in 1919 by the first of three generations of Whitehead's. Dr Brian Whitehead, Senior, was a man of many parts. He had served in the Royal Medical Corps during the 1914-18 war for which he was awarded the Military Cross.

He was in to every part of Downton life. Conjuror, actor, producer of several plays and variety shows, he was still actively doctoring in the village until after the Second World War. Then he was joined and succeeded by his son, another Brian, who was equally involved in the life of the community. He in turn was joined by Dr Alec Soutar in 1951.

Doctor Whitehead

In 1974, Dr Howgrave-Graham joined the practice and it is he who now leads the team of four doctors who look after 7,000 patients as the millennium ends.

For a time Dr Miranda Whitehead joined her father and she, too, became very involved in village life. Some of her playlets for the 1994 Downton Pageant have been included earlier in this book.

Hamilton House

At some point between 1945 and 1951 the surgery moved from an outhouse attached to Hamilton House, in Doctor's Alley, to the cottage the other side of Hamilton House, to the wooden hut which is at present the Library and then to the present Surgery in Moot Lane, purpose built in 1983 and extended in 1997.

CLUBS, SOCIETIES, ORGANISATIONS...

One of the tests of an active, lively village is the number of different interests it serves. At a recent count there were well over fifty different groupings with their own officers, committees, funds and organisation. It is almost invidious to single out any but the Womens' Institute is a bit special. It was formed in 1916, during the First World War, and was the first in Wiltshire.

Moot Lane Surgery

FIRE SERVICE

With so many thatched and wood-framed houses, fire must always have been a hazard. Downton had a fire engine at least from 1768 - it is in Salisbury Museum - and it was kept in the church, then in the National School, now the Church Hall. The Borough also had one and it gave endless trouble at the end of the 19th Century. A fire at the Agricultural College in 1891 had evidently exposed its failings so a new one was bought.

The old engine was moved to the Memorial Hall and the new machine was kept for a time near Iron Bridge. The Tannery had its own fire-fighting arrangements from 1919 with a stationary steam driven pump to supply sprinklers and heavy leather hoses (what else?!)

In 1940 a powerful portable appliance was obtained and during the war there was both a fire engine and an ambulance in the village.

From 1989 the Tannery employees crewed a well-equipped fire-engine. They were trained by Salisbury Fire Service and had weekly practice runs. At present the village is without a crew or machine.

The British Legion continues to support those who served their country and their families. It is also a club for a dwindling, ageing group of Ex-Servicemen who were in the wars of this century.

There are three football clubs with the oldest founded in 1895 and fielding three teams. The senior team had a particularly rosy patch between 1952 and 1961. In those nine years they won the Bournemouth Senior League no fewer than seven times.

Another centenarian is the Downton Cricket Club which has a rule that 60% of its players must be on the Downton Electoral Roll. Other big clubs with over 100 members are the Downton Bowling Club and the Downton Angling Club. The Downton Lawn Tennis Club has over 200 members, young and old.

Finally, there is the Downton Band. Founded in 1870 as the White Horse Orchestra it maintains a very high standard as it performs for various charitable fund-raising events.

LIBRARY

'November 10th, 1926. Mr Scott, schoolmaster, informed the Parish Council that it was intended to open a branch of the County Library in the Council School, Gravel Close.'

This operated for many years but the Wilts County Library is now housed in a wooden shed next to the Church Rooms in Snail Creep.

At its peak, in 1986, out of perhaps 600 competing in the annual National Brass Band Championships, Downton Band may have been the 27th best brass band in England. The Band plays carols through the village every Christmas morning from 4 a.m. to 7.30 a.m. and has done for 100 years.

CULTURAL LIFE

Downton has for long enjoyed a variety of cultural and social activities. Pageants, pantomimes, children's plays and carnivals are a recurring theme. There are also frequent fund-raising events like bazaars, jumble sales and bring-and-buy. Many of these take place at the centre of the village in the Memorial Hall. The Hall has progressed from its conversion to a Public Hall after the British School closed.

After each World War the Hall has been further developed. It now has a good stage with kitchen and lavatories and changing rooms. Further improvements are needed and are planned. Every Friday the Memorial Hall has the Women's Institute Market which attracts a wide circle of customers and an outlet for the cake-making, plant growing and clothes-making skills of WI Market members.

Other WI groups meet in the Hall. An art group, badminton club and horticultural club are regular users and the recent innovation of bringing in theatrical and musical groups seems to meet a need. One especial favourite is Forest Forge, a roving repertory group of professional actors who bring their own stage and set.

Chapter 14 Downton ready for its next Millennium

WHAT OF THE GREAT HOUSES AS THE MILLENNIUM ENDS?

Chalkhill House, the old Vicarage, is home for three generations. Mr and Mrs Peach have been active in local and county politics for many years.

Longford Castle remains the home of the Earls of Radnor and the centre of a great estate, the main 12,000 acres of which extends to Downton and beyond.

Moot House is in private ownership with the Creswell family involved in the worlds of finance and of embroidery.

New Court is the family home of the Hon. Peter Pleydell-Bouverie, a younger son of the Earl of Radnor.

Newhouse is the home of Mr and Mrs Jeffreys. George Jeffreys is a descendant of the Eyres who have had the house since 1633. They make it available for social and commercial functions.

Parsonage Manor, beautifully restored, is the family home of Mr and Mrs Hsuan and their three daughters. He is a mining entrepreneur, often abroad.

Trafalgar Park was bought by Mr Michael Wade who has put it in to a Trust. He has done a great deal of work to restore it. It is used for functions as well as musical events and filming.

Five years before the end of the millennium, a fine new sports hall and leisure centre has filled many of the gaps that the Memorial Hall could not cover. At a cost of over £500,000 the Brian Whitehead Leisure Centre has opened with indoor tennis, badminton and keep-fit facilities. Alongside it are the football ground, tennis courts and bowls green with clubhouse which were earlier phases of Downton's sporting evolution.

As the century ends, Downton has had its first visit by the Royal Shakespeare Company. They presented *Troilus and Cressida* and *A Month in the Country*. The company converted the new Leisure Centre to a stage for just a week.

They came in ignorance that ninety years ago Sybil Thorndike, one of the first great Dames of English theatre, was playing Downton in *Comedy of Errors* in the Moot.

She would have much enjoyed the irony that, with all the RSC's superb modern technical equipment creating a theatre with its seating, lighting, stage and settings, the weather, which had so plagued her visit, again intervened.

Chris Pitts
Cuckoo Fair's
inspiration over many
years

First torrential rain drowned out the spoken word and then lightning cause the lights to fail! She would have admired the way in which they coped. For Downton, 'though, it was a privilege to have such a disciplined and intelligent team of performers.

DOWNTON AND CUCKOOS

Why cuckoo ? There are many stories and any of them could be true. Here is one. In the 1930's a youth from Downton was apprenticed to a builder in Odstock. Knowing he was from Downton they would tease him, saying: 'Have they let the cuckoo out yet?' The boy's father told him this went back to the old Downton sheep fairs. When two shepherds were mocking a third for stupid behaviour they would call out: 'He's letting the cuckoo out!'

THE CUCKOO FAIR

The Borough was created in 1209 as a centre for trade. A Thursday market ran for many years and annual Fairs date back to the Borough's early days. Peddlers set up their stalls and cattle were sold at the Fair in April; sheep and horses were traded n September or October. They were also 'Hiring Fairs' for men seeking work. The Spring Fairs were often called Cuckoo Fairs. They were held on or near 23rd April.

The Downton Fairs stopped in 1914 at the start of the Great War and although briefly restarted after that War the village does not seem to have had the heart for it and they stopped. In 1980, whilst looking for ways to raise money for charities and clubs, the idea of reviving Cuckoo Fairs was raised. That touched a pleasure spot in Downton with its ever-present urge to enjoy itself.

The Cuckoo Princess is crowned with Downton lace

Now held every year on the Saturday nearest May Day, there are over 200 stalls with visitors coming from all over the south of England. Maypole and Morris dancers, clowns and conjurors, bands and combos entertain the milling throng which stays steady at about 15,000, year by year.

DOWNTON GROWS

Castle Meadow - where the first people lived

Joanna Close and Catherine Crescent

Secondary Modern School and the Industrial Estate

The population of the village over the centuries has fluctuated between 1,000 and nearly 4,000 (in 1851) but the rapid increase in the second half of the 20th Century was unprecedented and partly due to the motor car.

In 1931 there were only 1,350 people living in the village; by 1961 the population had increased to 1,800 in 550 households. By 1991 there were 2,800 living in 1,141 homes. A doubling of houses in 30 years.

Some of that increase came because homeless people, many of them coming back from the 1939-45 war, occupied the empty tin huts left by the American army. The huts were not designed for permanent use and so there was an urgent need to re-house the people, some of them squatters, living in very primitive conditions.

To take all these extra households, Downton had to expand. The main growth was at the two ends of the village, leaving the Borough and High Street, the old village in the middle, to absorb just a few of the new buildings.

That expansion was made possible by very practical changes - the running of both fresh water mains and sewage drains in the 1950's. In 1931 a man wanting to build his own house would choose low lying Charlton where fresh water could be had by digging only a shallow well rather than Moot Lane where a deep well would have been needed.

For most of its long story, if you lived in Downton you worked in Downton or close by. Indeed hamlets like Standlynch, Witherington and Charlton may well have been developed by the Bishops so that their workers could live closer to their work and did not need to travel from Downton. As the Millennium ends, 95% of those who live in Downton, and have work, travel away from the village to do it.

With the growth in numbers there came a need for bigger schools. The newly built Secondary Modern school off the Breamore Road opened in the '60s. That allowed the Church of England Primary School to move down from Barford Lane in to the Gravel Close school buildings.

The Primary School has over 200 children, aged 5 - 11, and 9 teachers. The Secondary School, 11 - 16 years, has nearly 300 pupils and 25 teachers. Post-16, most students go in to Salisbury. All this is a far cry from the 12 poor boys who studied in South Lane and the few who went to College in Winchester.

DOWNTON COPES

Downton has absorbed its extra people. The benefits of good schools, doctors, dentists, and a wide range of shops and services outweigh the crowded roads and the need to work away from the village.

Interestingly, a bid by Lord Radnor's estate to build another 400 houses in Downton west of the main north-south road, with the strong likelihood that that number would grow eventually to 1,000 - another doubling of population - ran into strong opposition from a wide cross-section of those living in Downton.

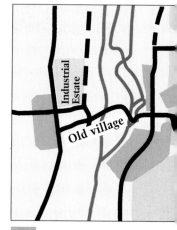

New housing

It will be for historians to disentangle how and why this change in mood, this 'thus far and no further' resistance by previously passive or accepting villagers, came about. The long drawn out battle over ten years through Planning refusal, Appeals, Inspector's Report and Appeal to the House of Lords ended in victory, at least for the time being, for those who thought change had gone far enough.

Some of the opposition undoubtedly came from people who had come to live in Downton because it was a comfortable village to live in and it seemed under threat. That may explain the incomers' reaction but history may look for a deeper, older, sadder explanation for the resistance of those who had and have long ties with the area. Memories are long in country places. When events of 190 years earlier can produce an explosive outburst from a villager it is evident that time in Downton is a slow healer. A suitable subject for someone's PhD, perhaps.

PROTECTING DOWNTON

History may look on the late 20th Century obsession with conservation as another example of the failure of the chattering classes to face and deal with the real challenges of global warming, technological revolution, over-population, poverty, disease and famine facing our world.

On the other hand those living in Downton can take comfort from the many designations which surround, almost cocoon, a lovely old village.

Downton is either in or bordering on an Area of Outstanding Natural Beauty, a Special Landscape Area, a Site of Special Scientific Interest (this is the whole Avon valley), a Conservation Area (the centre of the village), a European Special Area of Conservation and an Area of Special Archaeological Significance.

Over 100 herons and nearly 40 swans testify that the watermeadows and river, at least, are in a good state.

Many houses are listed as of architectural and historic interest and Downton is on the edge of the New Forest Heritage Area.

Downton's own practical conservation measures include the Moot Preservation Trust, which has transformed the badly neglected 11 acres of the Moot, and the Downton Millennium Green which will conserve and open to the public a meadow by the river along Moot Lane. The Downton Society attempts to act as guardian and watchdog to alert the village to new threats. It recently prepared the Downton Village Design Statement to help developers work in harmony with all that is best in the village.

CHANGE IS THE NAME OF THE GAME

As we move from one ever-changing century to the next it is good to gauge just how different things have become in Downton. Television, mobile 'phones, the Internet, the airliner and the car ensure that Downton can never ever again be a sleepy hollow cut off from the outside world. Homeworking is more widespread in the village than many realise and perhaps this will be the trend for villages like Downton.

This is end-of-century Downton: ordinary people made continuously aware of the world outside Downton whether it be pondering the virtues of the Euro, devolution by Scotland and Wales or being confronted daily with conflict in Eastern Europe and globally.

THE CHURCH UNCHANGING?

At first sight, the churches and chapels are the most unchanging part of Downton. However, religion, too, has changed. It is having to adapt to a community with very different values. One in three marriages end in divorce, sexual unorthodoxy is no longer socially unacceptable and women have rightly claimed an equality with men that the old hierarchy did not foresee.

The churches are having to find new answers, as is Society. All denominations now worship together from time to time. This new teamwork is worth keeping.

END OF A MILLENNIUM, START OF A NEW ONE

Downton has been fortunate. It has survived and more than survived. It has changed with the times and yet kept its sense of community and stability. The crew who gathered to plan Downton's millennial celebrations surprised each other with the variety of interests they represented. Downton is a friendly village where all are accepted and valued.

Its pattern of life today would be hardly intelligible to those first, skin-covered huntsmen and they would marvel at our comforts. However, at the heart of those early, pioneering men was the spirit of enterprise and adventure we have inherited.

We can but hope they would see that spirit in us as we go on in to our 8th Millennium. At least they would be happy that Downton still loves a party - the bigger, the better!

Acknowledgments
. . . and a small apology

Where to begin? With the apology, perhaps. There are almost no references. That is because almost all my sources are secondary. No-one can be expert over 7,000 years. I decided from the outset to rely on the experts, the specialists - as many as I could find - and to do no original research. Apart from one much enjoyed and appreciated morning in the company of Mrs Nancy Steele in the Muniments Room at Longford Castle after the book was virtually finished, I have stuck to that. Not one visit to the Public Records Office at Trowbridge but plenty to the public libraries, to the staff of which I am most grateful.

Five sources stand out. The *Victoria County History*, J H Bettey's *Wessex from 1,000 AD*, the many volumes produced by the Wiltshire Record Society, The Hatcher Review and A R Woodford's *History of Downton*. VCH gave the facts, Bettey gave perspective and the other three gave those little nuggets that bring history to life. The archaeological reports of Gibbs, Hinton and Rahtz have revealed a heritage far older and more interesting than was ever suspected by our forebears. Conrad Saunders' 'Downton's Richest Family' supplied most of the Duncombe material and an unpublished history of Downton Baptists held by the South Lane church was the basis for most of the study of Baptist development.

So many individuals have helped with anecdotes, documents and old pictures that I think it safer just to say a big 'Thank you' to you all! Four, however, must be mentioned.

Miranda Whitehead's playlets for the 1994 Downton Pageant remain vivid in the minds of all who watched it - and over half the village were involved. The first playlet is mine but the others follow hers closely.

John Snelgrove's researches into his own family in Downton have uncovered much new detail.

Ken Light's work on the Downton emigrants to Canada has told us about them but also much about life in Downton in the 1830's.

David Hyde's expertise on railway history has been invaluable.

Thank you all for letting us share.

Ruth and Ted Austen, Alex Belbin, Daphne Greville-Heygate, Joan Gwyther, Tony Howgrave-Graham, Barbara Newman and John Shave will recognise a good number of the photographs and other items we have used (the others are by me) and we are grateful to them. I use the plural 'we' because one of the delights for me and I hope for the reader has been the artistic flair of Jane Ancona (if you smile at a sketch it is probably by her and her cover paintings brilliantly set the stage for the book) and the design skill of Geoff Holland who, in many hours of disciplined creation, has brought it all together.

It has been fun lifting a potentially boring narrative with their help and bringing it to life. I would have been lost without them. We, in turn, know that the printing expertise of Keith Kirkland has ensured that Downton has a millennial marker to be proud of. We hope you enjoy the result.

The advertisers have 'paid' for the expensive colour section and left their topical marks for future generations to enjoy! Their contribution is much appreciated.

Lastly, this book might never have been published but for the lead given by Margaret Peach, currently Chairman of the Downton Parish Council, and the support of the Downton Millennium Celebration Committee and Downton village as a whole.

DAVID WAYMOUTH
Downton, August 1999

FAMILY NAMES THAT APPEAR IN THE 1599 REGISTER
AND ON THE 1999 ELECTORAL ROLL

Abbot	Compton	Fulford	Lane	Paine	Skeat
Aldridge	Cooper		Leicester	Palmer	Spencer
Austin	Coward	Glover	Lee	Parker	Spence
	Cowper	Greene	Lewis	Parkin	Steele
Barker	Crocker	Gifford	Light	Pearse	Steevens
Barter			Longe	Penny	Stoke
Bennett	Daniel	Hadley		Pinhorne	
Burke	Day	Harding	Merriefield	Plaskett	Tanner
Bishop	Deene	Haydon	Michell	Powell	
Blackwell	Downer	Higgins	Morris		Wall
Blake		Hill	Mowdy=	Read	Webb
Bromfield	Eastman	Hobbs	Moody	Reeves	Weeke
Bryant	Edwards	Humby	Musselwhite	Russell	Wheatley
Bundy	Eliot	Ireland			Whit=
	Evance=	Jeffrey	Nash	Savage	Witt=
Carter	Evans		Newman	Scoates	White?
Candy		Kent	Noble	Sevior	Whitmarsh
Chalke	Ford			Shepheard	Wilson
Collier	Fry	Lambe	Osmond	Singsburye	Wyatt

220 EMIGRANTS FROM DOWNTON TO ONTARIO, CANADA
AND 3 TO AUSTRALIA

The surnames of the families that emigrated from Downton to Canada in 1835 and 1836 are given below.

Alexander, Allen,Bampton,Barrow,Barter,Biddlecomb, Bishop, Chas. and E.Bundy 1835, Bundy,Chalk 1835, Chalk,Champ,Compton,Dale,Deere, Dredge,Eastman, Edmonds, Foe, Forder,Frampton, Friar, Futcher, Gauntlett, Gilbert, Goulding, Harrington, Harris, Higgs 1835, Higgs, Hudson, Jellyman, Jennings,King 1835, King, Latty, Light, Moody, Mussel, Noyse, Perry 1835, Poore, Pracey 1835, Pressy, Pretty, Prince, Shergold, Small, Swayne, Thorn, Webb, Weeks

These names have been provided by Ken Light who is himself descended from the 1836 emigrant group. He is always interested in information relating to the group and his E-mail address is ken_light@yahoo.com also look at http://www.geocities.com/athens/styx/2932/index.htm a website dedicated to the emigration to Lake Erie. Or write to Ken Light c/o Elgin Co. Ontario Genealogical Society, Box 20060, St Thomas, ON N5P 4H4 Canada or try bedmonds@ican.net

In 1851 the following emigrated to Australia: Arney, Fanstone, Poulton.

NAME MENTIONS:

Names without much information about them are listed below.

Alexander,141,	Fanstone,75,186,	Kelsey,86,	Quinton,113,
Ambrose,8,		King,127,	
Armney(Arney),129,186,	Gale,145,		Reffell,173,
	Gifford,146,	Langham,172,	Rhodes,122,
Baily,128,	Godwin,135,	Lawes,98,	Robinson,123,
Barrow,135,	Goldstone,64,	Lee,120,	
Bedoe,75,	Greene,89,	Lenthall,86,	St.Amand,89,
Blake,112,	Groone,141,	Littlecot,112,	Sheffield,172,
Boorn,126,			Sheppard,98,
Brandon,140,	Hamilton,47,	Maple,76,	Shilly,95,
Bunbury,148,	Harrison,157,	Matcham,127,	Smith,120,
Bundy,161,	Hayter,84,	Miles,112,	Snakenborg,101,
Burnell,48,	Hedda,24,	Miller,94,	Snowe,84,98,
	Hewett,146,	Mitchel,95,	
Chalk,82,98,112,	Hewson,86,	Moody,128,	Templemans,77,
Churchill,143,	Hibberd,141,		Thor,82,
Clarke,117,	Hickman,82,	Newman,113,	Thrings,77,
Cooper,112,	Hooper,85,	Nicholas,137,	Tiptaft,138,
Cox,145,	Hulse,79,	Noble,98,	
Creswell,178,	Hulton,91,	Noyce,157,	Webb,146,
Crisp,153,	Humby,141,	Noyes,116	Welstead,75,
			Weston,112,
Davies,77,	Janes,138,	Payne,129,144,	Wheeler,98,
Dove,95,	Jeffreys,178,	Pell,86,	White,91,
	Jellyman,121,	Pleydell-Bouverie,178,	Witt,120,
Elliott,120,	Jennings,74,	Plumptre,123,	Worral,113,
England,154	Justian,74,	Pope,141,	Wright,148,
		Poulton,133,	

Index